Mainly
for
Mothers

MAINLY FOR
MOTHERS

**A practical
discipleship
course**

WENDY VIRGO

Mainly
for
Mothers

Wendy Virgo

KINGSWAY PUBLICATIONS
EASTBOURNE

ISBN 0 85476 689 8

Text typesetting and cover design
supplied by Pinnacle Creative.

Print production by Bookprint Creative Services
P.O. Box 827, BN21 3YJ, England, for
KINGSWAY PUBLICATIONS LTD
Lottbridge Drove, Eastbourne, East Sussex, BN23 6NT.
Printed in Great Britain.

Contents

Introduction

It takes no special discernment to observe that our society is in a critical state. Daily, the media fling their disturbing information at us: abuse and brutality, murder and rape. Violence of every kind is common, and what is increasingly disturbing is the number of young offenders, even children not yet in their teens. Teachers are under attack literally, there is scant respect for the elderly, property gets vandalised, and parents wring their hands in helpless frustration. Everyone wants to blame someone else for the anarchy and chaos.

What we are seeing is the result of a world turning its back on godly principles of living. There are, of course, various reasons why this should be escalating at this particular time, but I believe that seeds were sown in the sixties, which was a very significant decade. A growing discontent among women gave rise to major changes in important areas. For example, their entrance into the workplace alongside men, the emergence of many into prominent leading roles in business and politics, equality of wage-earning potential, and increasing boldness to speak out on many issues.

The new winds that blew resulted in much-needed change. There were, however, also kick-backs. One of these has been a discontent with domesticity and a devaluing of motherhood. Another has been higher standards of living, resulting in greater demands for material things and, consequently, a conflict of priorities. Yet another has been greater strain on marriages. Many have cracked and fallen apart. Adjustments to divorce laws have made divorce more accessible and thereby blunted the inclination to work harder on the marriage relationship.

All this has contributed to a growing climate of instability and fragmentation. Secure families are the backbone of a stable nation; the breakdown of family life is both the root and the fruit of a sick society.

We believe that the gospel has power to change the individual and consequently to change society. But we need to know how to apply it specifically. People are being born again into God's kingdom who need help to discover his ways of building healthy marriages, homes and families.

One night I was praying about how best to help the young women in our church. I awoke in the 'small hours' with the reference Titus 2:3–5 impressed on my mind. When I looked it up I found a very succinct and practical blueprint for teaching certain skills. But it is also to do with relationship, for it instructs the 'older women' to train the 'younger women'. This is in accordance with Jesus' command to 'make disciples' of all nations.

These principles are not limited to one culture or era. In fact, these very Bible studies have been used effectively in America, Italy and India as well as England. They are not to be discarded as relevant only to the first century AD. They are not 'Western' or 'English', but biblical.

WHAT ARE PRINCIPLES?

This is an important question. Principles are not rules. Rules are rigid and permit no flexibility or interpretation. Principles are guidelines that help to define standards and values. Rules are like walls that fence you in to a restricted area; principles are like railway lines. They give a defined pathway for a potentially lethal locomotive to make progress safely. If it comes off the rails, it ceases to make progress and can cause a lot of damage to itself and others. But even on those guiding rails, trains go at different speeds; some stop at stations, and some pass straight through – so there is variety.

Rules tell me what to do, whereas principles tell me the best way to get somewhere, while giving me the dignity to make my own choices as I go. An example of a rule is: 'No Smoking.' An example of a principle is: 'I will not be mastered by anything.' I now have a reasoned choice about how I treat my body. If a substance is likely to master it, e.g. tobacco, it's sensible not to start using it. A principle is wider than a rule.

Why is it so important to spell this out? Because this book is not a rule book. It will not tell you exactly what you must do to be a good wife or mother. Every marriage is unique and so is every child. God does not want us to live by rules, but by relating to him. The Bible tells us what he likes and what works.

This book does not presume to be a comprehensive commentary on Titus 2:3–5, or a marriage guidance manual or a conclusive volume on child-raising. Its purpose is to put a tool in the hands of any woman who is concerned about how to get alongside another woman in order to help her to discover God's principles for building a stable home, to talk them through and put them into action.

WHO ARE THE PRINCIPLES FOR?

After writing to Titus that the older women are to teach the younger women, Paul then gives six basic areas of instruction, mainly to do with family life. 'Younger' and 'older' are relative terms and could mean 'less experienced' and 'more experienced'.

Women who are mothers are the main focus, but young women recently married or soon to be married could also benefit from these studies.

WHAT ABOUT SINGLE MOTHERS?

As the first instruction Paul gives to women in this passage is about loving their husbands, obviously this chapter will not apply to those without husbands. But I suggest the leader of the study could use the first week(s) to gently open up discussion about attitudes to men, fathers, commitment. This is probably better dealt with in a one-to-one setting, with more specialist material than this handbook provides. There may be a very bruised young woman sitting in front of you who needs careful loving help. On the other hand, she may simply be a product of modern thinking which has discarded marriage as irrelevant, and some guidance about what the Bible says may be appropriate.

With others, it may be best to go straight to Chapter 2, and pick up on personal feelings about relationships as you go along. Basically, play it by ear!

However, it is certain that any mother who finds herself raising a family on her own, for whatever reason, will need lots of support and friendship. Some churches have set up support groups especially for them which are very effective. Perhaps you could consider starting one in your church.

WHAT ABOUT WORKING MOTHERS?

Nowadays the assumption is that most wives and mothers will have a job outside the home. While it is understood that many are under severe financial pressure, and the mother may be the main or indeed the only breadwinner, let us not automatically assume that it is the best course to take. For some there is no choice – young couples today struggle with immense mortgages or extortionately high rents, and they have no option but to work long and hard hours – in which case there are big challenges to face with regard to juggling time and priorities.

But where there is the possibility of delaying a return to work or of doing without a job altogether while the children are little, this should be considered carefully. Our children need our undivided attention during their early years. We are breeding a nation of insecure children without strong family ties. Children who grow up in the care of minders without much interaction with their parents can be particularly vulnerable to fear, rejection and insecurity. Not only does it have implications for the children, but the mums can feel overstretched, and miss out on some of the unique joys of watching their children develop.

Above all, we need to see the crucial importance of our role in mothering which has been so drastically undermined, and adopt a positive attitude to it. This may mean postponing our career for a while or taking a part-time job instead of a full-time one, or even being content with a lower-grade one if that can give us more time with our child. But in the end we shall gain in terms of a more integrated, richer family life if we do it in faith.

However, where taking a job is necessary and unavoidable, we need sympathetic and practical help from one another, and this is an area where older 'mothers in Israel' can come alongside.

AN OUTLINE OF THE COURSE

There are six basic areas arranged in eight chapters:

1. How to love our husbands
2. How to love our children
3. Self-control
   Part One: The new self, controlled by truth
   Part Two: Action stations
4. The importance of the home
   Part One: The homemaker
   Part Two: The home
5. Kindness
6. Biblical submission
   Part One: What it is
   Part Two: Working it out

The lessons can be used in a group setting or one-on-one.

The first week will be an introduction to the course. I use this to set the mood of the sessions, i.e. friendly, informal, relaxed; to find out the names of those attending and something of their circumstances, for example, how long they have been Christians.

I also use it to establish that the Bible is our authority and reveals how God wants us to live as Christian women. It sets out principles, but there is plenty of scope for interpreting and using those principles. I try to aim for an open, relaxed atmosphere where discussion is very much encouraged.

The chapter on loving our children inevitably takes a lot of time – sometimes several weeks – but I would advocate not getting stuck on it indefinitely, as we also need to enlarge and consider wider aspects of home life. Also, the lessons often overlap and you will find that we come back to child-raising issues again and again.

Practical sessions

Chapter 4 ends with some practical suggestions about organising housework, and housekeeping money. It can be fun and constructive to build in a week or two at this point when the group takes a break from the study and meets to swap money-saving ideas, outgrown baby clothes, jewellery and new things to do with pasta! Also hunt out books that you can recommend and lend out.

A NOTE ON 'OLDER WOMEN'

There are many wise and experienced women in the body of Christ who have successfully raised families and have (or have had) good strong marriages.

Sadly it is often the case that women who have devoted themselves to raising their children and homemaking, out of the conviction that this was right, find themselves in a quandary in their middle years. Their *raison d'être* is no longer obvious with their children less dependent, and it can be difficult to enter or re-enter the work force at this stage (especially without a degree or training). So a sense of purposelessness can creep over their lives. From being the focal point of a busy family, a woman can feel sidelined and redundant.

Hormonal changes may coincide, compounding feelings of depression. The verve and vigour of her earlier years have diminished but are not totally extinguished; the frustrating feeling that a lot of time has gone by and there is proportionately little left in which to realise her hopes and dreams results in panic and desperation.

Women who have been pursuing a successful career may find other challenges coincide with a time when they are feeling less on top emotionally and physically. Can they keep up with new techniques and trends? Can they cope with the demands of a family and possibly aging parents while conscious of younger, competitive colleagues breathing down their necks? All this and hot flushes too!

Accepting that one is middle-aged requires a huge gear-shift mentally and emotionally. Many accomplish it with barely a change of pace, making the transition easily and naturally from one stage to another. Many do not. For them the shift of gears is clumsy and jerky, accompanied by harsh screeching from a protesting gear-box. They get through it, but the mechanism is rather damaged.

Women knew nothing about cars in Paul's day of course, and probably few had careers (although some did – Lydia for example). But they surely experienced the menopause, even if they did not have a name for it! Paul observed that some women of his acquaintance were irreverent in their behaviour. It may have been the mixture of hormonal changes, family disruption and middle-aged frustration which led them to become somewhat cynical and disillusioned. Unable to resort to Valium, some hit the bottle and became 'addicted to much wine'; and some with time on their hands now that their families had grown, buzzed around indulging in malicious gossip.

Maybe poor overworked Titus had confided in Paul that he didn't know how he could care for this group of people. Meanwhile, lots of young women were getting saved and he was at his wits' end trying to teach them. Paul's solution was simple. As an overworked pastor, Titus would do well to release men and women in all age groups to teach what they had learned.

Paul recognised that a wealth of experience and wisdom was locked up in these older women. Let them get alongside the younger ones and encourage them; acknowledge their gifting. Some would be practical and motherly, and others more methodical teachers, but let them pass on principles tried and tested, founded on the word of God.

I am not suggesting, of course, that all the complex feelings of the middle-age syndrome will be alleviated by starting a study group! But where a mother feels her motherly activities and fulfilment are petering out, she may find a whole new avenue of invaluable service opening up as she begins to lend a sympathetic ear, a helping hand and the benefit of her experience to a younger woman (or women). There is a crying need for someone to get alongside young women who have recently become Christians and have no idea how to be godly wives and mothers. *This is nothing less than a call to discipleship.* Jesus commanded us to go and make disciples. I believe he is looking for 'mothers in Israel' who will use the wealth of wisdom they have acquired to disciple younger women.

BUT WHAT IF I'M A FAILURE?

Some will feel disqualified because their own marriages are or were broken or less than perfect, or their children were not exemplary. To be honest, that applies to just about everyone! But if they have come through their experiences with humility, grace and dignity, others can profit by them. It is often easier to relate to someone who is willing to be vulnerable and share her mistakes to help others avoid them, than to someone who appears never to have put a foot wrong.

MOTHERS IN ISRAEL

Once, during a time of ministry, I had a vision. I could see a hill and at the top was a well. Over it was a roof supported by a circle of pillars. In between each pillar stood a woman. I looked down the hill and saw numerous people streaming up. They were in all sorts of conditions: dirty, ragged, hungry and thirsty, lame, sick. As they came up, the women stepped forward from between the pillars and with hands outstretched advanced to meet them. Gently and lovingly, they escorted them to the well, where they helped them to drink and cleaned them up. It was the water they needed. The women knew where it was and helped them get to it.

Revival is coming, when myriads are going to be pressing in to the kingdom. There will be multitudes of needs – healing, cleansing, deliverance, teaching – among all categories of people. One of those needs will be to disciple and encourage young mothers.

I hope this book will be a useful tool. I see it as part of the preparation for revival.

Recommended Reading
MacDonald, Gordon. *Living at High Noon*. Marc Europe

Chapter 1

Setting the scene

You may be wondering: who was Titus? Why did the apostle Paul write him a letter, and what has it got to do with me?

Titus was a friend and travelling companion of the apostle Paul. He was one of Paul's converts, and he may have been the brother of Luke who wrote the Gospel of Luke, and the book of Acts. Paul refers to him as 'my partner and fellow-worker' and entrusted him with delivering his second epistle to the church in Corinth, and also with raising contributions to a famine-relief fund for suffering Christians in Jerusalem.

Wherever Paul went he preached the gospel. On one occasion he was shipwrecked on the island of Crete. Some people became believers when he shared the gospel with them and a church began to form. Paul left Titus there to establish the work and appoint elders. In this letter Paul tells him what qualities to look for in potential elders, but it was not only elders who were to teach, encourage and disciple. Paul wanted everyone to be involved – older men and women, younger men and women, even the slaves. He urged them all to lead godly lives that demonstrated God's grace.

Our studies are based on Paul's advice to Titus on how to treat and encourage the women:

Older women likewise are to be reverent in their behavior, not malicious gossips, nor enslaved to much wine, teaching what is good, that they may encourage the young women to love their husbands, to love their children, to be sensible, pure, workers at home, kind, being subject to their own husbands that the word of God may not be dishonored (Titus 2:3–5, NASB).

THE OLDER WOMEN

One wonders why Paul particularly selected these faults in verse 3. Perhaps he had specific women in mind who were not a blessing to the church but an obstruction as they idled away their time drinking and gossiping. Maybe they were sad and lonely and needed a sense of purpose, as we saw in the introductory chapter.

On the other hand, he evidently met women who were such good examples that he felt they were worthy role models. Perhaps he had stayed in Christian houses on his travels and found them to be places of refuge and contentment because the wife and mother was so loving and wise. How important the influence of such women was in the church! For as they gave themselves to their husbands and families, they brought honour to the word of God.

QUESTIONS

1. What is 'honouring the word of God'? How do you 'honour' anyone? Maybe words like 'respect', 'obey', 'place a high value on' spring to mind. Discuss how we could apply them to the word of God.

2. How important is it to do this?

3. From this passage, how could I as a Christian woman dishonour the word of God??

We could have many motives for doing a study like this; for example, to gain some tips on child-rearing or brightening up a flagging marriage; to debate with other women about our roles, or even to find out if there is a certain 'image' to which we should conform.

Ask yourself: Is it my desire to honour Jesus by obedience to his word?

The word of God brings clarity. It is like a lamp that shows the way, and like a plumb-line that shows where we are crooked. Let us approach it with a humble attitude and an open heart that is willing to learn (Col 3:16; Jn 14:15).

Recommended Reading
Yates, John & Susan. *What Really Matters at Home*. Word UK

Chapter 2

How to love our husbands

It may seem strange that older women are urged to train the younger ones to love their husbands. Doesn't love come naturally? Surely if they have to be told to do it, there isn't much hope! Let's talk about love.

1. Love is to do with the mind as well as the emotions

It is to do with commitment, self-denial and right decisions, as well as feelings of romance, desire and passion.

Dr Martyn Lloyd-Jones said, 'Many marriages break down because people do not realise what love means.' Because by nature human beings are selfish we have to cultivate love deliberately. True love is unselfish, and puts other people's interests before our own (read 1 Corinthians 13).

2. Love is not passive

Falling in love seems to just 'happen' to us, but maintaining love requires determination and effort. Love must be declared, and it is important to be able to say, 'I love you,' and to say it often. But the declaration must be followed with demonstration. As Eliza Doolittle demands in *My Fair Lady*, 'Don't give me words: Show me!' The greatest display of love in history is God's love to us in Jesus, who gave his life for us to rescue us from sin and death (Rom 5:8). We can only continue to *give* love as we keep on receiving God's love.

3. The difference between God's love and human love

God's love for us is entirely unconditional. That is, it is not based on how good or clever or attractive we are. We cannot earn it.

QUESTION

Look up Deuteronomy 7:7. Why did God love Israel?

Human love fluctuates and changes. Sometimes we feel loving. Sometimes we mistake sympathy for love; sometimes we do 'loving' things in order to get our own way. Often we mistake sexual desire for love. Love for our husbands includes all these elements of sympathy, doing loving things, and physical desire. But our pattern must be God's love which is never manipulative, self-seeking or demanding.

WHAT DID GOD INTEND MARRIAGE FOR (GENESIS 2:18–25)?

1. Companionship (v.18)
2. Partnership
3. Exclusive commitment
4. Sexual intimacy
5. Creating families

Now let's look at these one by one.

1. Companionship

Adam was incomplete and lonely on his own. He needed someone to share his life, to help him and encourage him. God made Eve to be a 'helper, suitable to him'. Sadly the word 'helper' has been put down and interpreted to mean inferior or secondary. God never intended Eve to be seen in this way. Indeed, he himself is often spoken of as our help; the Holy Spirit is called the Helper, the one who comes alongside.

God did not create another man to be Adam's helper, but a woman: different yet corresponding to him. She was to be a friend in a unique way.

QUESTIONS

1. **Could I describe myself as my husband's friend? Do we share our lives – e.g. interests, hopes and dreams, disappointments, thoughts and feelings – as well as more practical things like maintaining the house and how we use our money?**

2. **Do we try to make time just to be together?**

3. **Am I his 'helper'? Do I make his life easier or more difficult?**

4. **How do I feel about being a helper to him? Why?**

5. **Do we have fun together?**

---

2. Partnership

God gave Adam a job to do (v.15): to cultivate the garden. He also gave him a command to obey (vv.16–17): not to eat of the tree of knowledge of good and evil. Eve, as his 'helper', was to support him and help him to carry out God's plan.

Basically, God's will for us is to see his kingdom established on earth, as we grow more and more like Jesus, and live lives pleasing to him. Ideally, a husband and wife are to be a team – partners in working out God's plans. Pray that your husband will love God with all his heart and will have the courage to obey him. Even if your husband is not a Christian, you can start praying this for him. (See Matthew 6:10,33; 2 Corinthians 5:8–9; Colossians 1:9–11.)

Eve failed in her role to help her husband do God's will. In fact she helped him to sin.

QUESTIONS

1. **Am I making it easier for my husband to obey God, or am I obstructing him?**

2. **In what other ways can I see myself and my husband as partners?**

3. **What goals does he have? How can I encourage him in these?**

4. **What goals do I have? Can I share them with him?**

---

3. Exclusive commitment (Genesis 2:24; Psalm 45:10)

(a) When a man and woman marry, they separate themselves from their parents. Their primary commitment is no longer to their mother and father, but to the new partner. Together they form a new unit – 'one flesh'. It is important to understand this. Many parents are reluctant to let their children go and want to retain their hold upon their 'little boy' or 'little girl', not recognising that with marriage the childhood is ended, and a subtle change takes place.

Similarly the son or daughter must put their wife/husband first or they could be confused about where their duty lies and be vulnerable to guilt and manipulation.

Think about this. Who do you put first – your husband or your mother? Do you constantly compare your husband with your father? There must be a 'leaving' mentally and emotionally from our parents and a 'cleaving'; that is, a joining to our husbands.

At the same time, we must remember that we are to honour our parents all through our lives (Ex 20:12; Eph 6:2).

(b) One flesh: When a husband and wife are joined sexually, in God's eyes they are now a unit. In today's sexual climate, where fidelity is taken lightly or even despised, people are unaware of the trauma that results when a partner sleeps with someone else. It can have physical repercussions, but it will certainly bring emotional confusion, guilt and pain. When a woman gives herself to a man, she gives her soul as well as her body. She 'belongs' to her husband. So to commit adultery plunges her into an identity crisis and breaks the bond of trust with her husband. Biological union implies a spiritual and relational union.

QUESTIONS

1. Have I cut the 'umbilical cord' between myself and my parents?

2. Does my husband know that he is the only one in my life, and that I intend to keep it that way?

3. How do I view my marriage vows?

---

4. Sexual intimacy

Adam and Eve were naked, yet were not ashamed (Gen 2:25). God intended us to have a healthy enjoyment of one another's bodies. It is good to know that sexual love with our husbands is enjoyable, and right and acceptable to God! God invented it and wants us to enjoy it fully.

The Song of Songs is a celebration of sexual love between a couple committed to and infatuated with each other. Through the ages some people have been puzzled by its inclusion in the Holy Scriptures and have attempted to spiritualise it. Undoubtedly one can find valid parallels in our fellowship with the Lord Jesus, and it can be used as a parable of Christ's love for the church, but nowhere does it say that, and it is quite proper to take it at its face value – a love poem.

This shows us first that *sexual love is highly regarded by God*. A whole book is devoted to it! There it is sandwiched between Ecclesiastes and Isaiah, equal to them in wisdom, importance and divine inspiration.

Second, *our bodies are to be appreciated not despised*. Some religions and philosophies teach that the body is not to be honoured. For example, Buddhism says that evil resides in the body and true spiritual fulfilment can only be achieved when the body is totally subdued and ceases to influence us. The Greek Stoics taught that the body was to be rigorously disciplined and controlled, and that the intellect was superior to the physical. Medieval monks wore hair shirts, and practised flagellation (beating themselves) in order to chasten and subdue bodily cravings.

On the other hand, Epicureans believed in luxury and sensual pleasure as being the way to fulfilment, and hedonism is the philosophy that pleasure is the principal good.

Both views focus on the body.

Of all faiths, Christianity gives us the most healthy perspective: we honour the Lord Jesus in our spirits and minds, and let him rule over our bodies.

The body, then, is elevated in importance as a vehicle for working out God's purposes, but not to be given over to sensuality and gratification for its own sake. It is not good or bad, but neutral. It is to be honoured as God's workmanship and a temple of the Holy Spirit, but not worshipped. See 1 Corinthians 6:19–20. (We will look at this more fully at the end of Chapter 4.)

Sexual intercourse is intended to be the highest pinnacle of a man and woman's love for each other. It is not supposed to be the first thing they do together, but the consummation of a love that already exists, has been declared and has grown over a period of time in an exclusive relationship. It is much more than a biological union. It is an expression of love at its deepest level, and involves the emotions, will and spirit as well as the physical body.

It is also the outworking of a covenant between the husband and wife; and each bind themselves into a commitment that they will never do this with anyone else as long as they both shall live.

Born-again Christians have the capacity to have the most fulfilling sexual relationships of all human beings! This is not because we know all the answers, but because we have a new heart, and our minds are being renewed. So our past, with all its wrong perspectives, shame and guilt, no longer needs be a barrier to freedom in this area. As we let Jesus progressively change us, we will find that his truth sets us free to love each other without fear, guilt, embarrassment or reluctance.

As God's love works in us we are released to seek one another's happiness and are no longer bound to the treadmill of trying to find self-fulfilment. As we do this, we find we are more fulfilled ourselves. We are designed to be givers as well as receivers.

READ

Proverbs 5:15–23; 31:12; Ephesians 5:28; Hebrews 13:14.

(a) Sexual fulfilment
Many people are fairly shy about discussing this with anyone, husbands included. But God has put us together in covenant

relationships, and, just as we need to practise loving each other in other ways, so we need to practise talking about sexual intimacy. Perhaps the most important thing we have to learn to do is to talk about what turns us on.

Do not be afraid to say what you like your husband to do, and ask him what he likes, at all stages of sexual intimacy. If you feel embarrassed about this, it might help to talk when the lights are out. And don't forget, there are non-verbal ways of communicating enjoyment as well! The more open and honest you are with one another in these areas of physical intimacy, the more pleasure you will give and receive.

It takes time to develop a satisfying sexual relationship. Give each other time to learn and enjoy discovering what makes the other tick.

(b) Men and women are different

You know how it goes – the wife wanders across the bedroom in her underwear thinking, 'Where did I leave my book?' when hey presto – the husband sees her, and sight arouses feelings!

At this point remember that he is not being inconsiderate or thoughtless. He is reacting as God designed him – as a mortal male. However inconvenient, it is a moment to rejoice. He loves you (Prov 5:15–19). You are a gift from God to him. Learning to recognise and understand the differences in attitude between men and women helps enormously in lessening the misunderstanding and tensions that can occur.

A man's response is faster than a woman's. He is more often first aroused by sight; she by sound and touch. Don't worry if the wife needs time to be aroused. This is normal. It teaches the husband to be patient and loving (Eph 5), putting his wife's interests before his own. Romance keeps sexual intimacy alive.

(c) Reassurance

Sexual intimacy is often a wonderful way of being told, 'I love you, even if you've had an awful day.' Husbands need reassurance. Conflicts can often be resolved between you in this context; as you talk closely, it puts things into perspective. Forgiveness is easier.

(d) Comfort
It does not always have to be earth-shaking! This kind of intimacy can often be tender and emotionally satisfying when either of you feels hurt or worried. Husbands need comfort (even if sometimes they are not aware of their need!).

(e) Closeness
Your spouse is the person God gave you to bless you and for you to bless. Closeness in a good loving relationship is very therapeutic. It re-establishes your marriage vows: 'Love him, honour him, comfort him, and keep him, in sickness and in health, and forsaking all other, keep thee only unto him, as long as ye both shall live.'

(f) A command
The husband should give to his wife her conjugal rights, and likewise the wife to her husband. For the wife does not rule over her own body, but the husband does; likewise the husband does not rule over his own body, but the wife does (1 Cor 7:3–5. Do not refuse one another, except perhaps by agreement for a season.)

(g) A safeguard
Sex is a significant way in which we can help our husbands avoid sexual temptation (1 Cor 7:5) and sin. In a Christian marriage it is good to make love whenever you feel like it, but also at times when you do not.

Possible hindrances to sexual fulfilment:

(a) Shame
If you are ashamed of your body, it might well inhibit your enjoyment of love-making. Self-disgust can destroy your

happiness and cast doubt on your confidence to satisfy your husband. Maybe you need to talk and pray about this with a friend or counsellor if this is your problem.

(b) Fear of losing control
Inhibitions are usually the result of fears deep within of losing control. Many of us unconsciously harbour the fear that the worst thing we can do is to let go. We have nurtured a belief that we must be in control of the situation, ourselves and our emotions, and if that control seems threatened we panic.

(c) Past abuse
Others fear sexual intimacy because of abuse in the past. The very one(s) who should have protected and shielded them have wounded and betrayed them. Now confronted by a loving husband who also should be a shield and protector they find it difficult to entrust themselves for fear of further betrayal and disappointment.

(d) Guilt
Another factor is an enormous weight of guilt which can be generated through past abuse or previous affairs.

(e) Fear of failure
Fear of failure is another barrier to sexual happiness.

(f) Anger
Others are full of anger and hatred generated by being violated by a man or men who have had their pleasure without any sense of responsibility.

(g) Fatigue
Other less crucial barriers to sexual satisfaction are fatigue, illness and worry. Small children, lack of sleep, teenagers coming home late and pressures at work can all be hindrances to sexual intimacy.

If we are to really love our husbands, we must work at the intimate side of marriage. Therefore if any of these problems apply to us, we must give serious time and attention to facing up to them, with a view to receiving healing where necessary, and making adjustments.

TO DO

Take time to talk and pray through the relevant areas with a trusted counsellor and/or friend.

---

5. Creating families

Lastly, marriage was created to provide a secure environment in which to raise the next generation. This is obviously something that a husband and wife must share in. A wife shows her love to her husband by supporting him in his role of authority in the home, and by fulfilling her own caring, mothering role. But let us be careful that we don't get so absorbed in mothering that our husbands get neglected and shut out.

Read Proverbs 31:10–12,30. Here is a happy wife. Her husband trusts her, loves her and praises her. 'She brings him good, not harm, all the days of her life.' Her whole life is orientated towards serving him: to building him up, supporting and encouraging him.

What a risk! Surely she must be a down-trodden, exploited doormat? As we continue in our studies we shall see that that is the last thing God wants us to be.

Recommended Reading

LaHaye, Tim & Beverley. *The Act of Marriage*. HarperCollins
Wilthew, John & Liz. *Honouring Marriage*. Word UK

Chapter 3

How to love our children

Please bear in mind that this is a huge subject and we cannot hope to cover it completely here. Nevertheless, I hope that the principles discussed in this section will give us some useful guidelines. You may not find every part is relevant to you (or your group).

LOVING OUR CHILDREN

Why would we need to be taught this? Isn't it instinctive for mothers to love their children?

As we saw in the previous lesson, human love can be an inadequate, devious thing, and what seems to be love can actually be a disguise for something much less attractive. What appears to be maternal love can actually be:

1. Fear
(a) Fear of losing control: seen in being dominating.
(b) Fear of sickness or accident: seen in being over-protective.
(c) Fear of failure as a mother: anger at the child's failure to reach the mother's expectations.
(d) Fear of losing child's affection: seen in over-indulgence and weak discipline.

2. Ignorance

Ignorance of a child's basic needs. For example, valuing education as a top priority; having equipment, toys, etc., when the child's deepest need is for intimate, trusting relationships.

3. Self-protection

Having too little discipline, thinking that if I'm strict they won't love me. Or having too much discipline, in order to uphold my reputation and identity.

As we have seen, the essence of genuine love is self-giving.

THINGS I NEED TO KNOW ABOUT MYSELF

1. I will never be a perfect mother. When I had my first baby I initially felt terrified at the huge responsibility I had for this helpless infant. Then, believing motherhood to be part of God's plan for my life, I determined to be the best mother I possibly could be – a laudable ambition. But I soon exhausted myself trying to be a perfect mother, and disappointed myself that I could not reach my self-appointed goal. Not only was I not a perfect mother, but my child was not a perfect child!

If our goal is to be a perfect mother we will fail; we will disappoint ourselves, and get angry with our children for causing us to fail!

Pursue excellence, but not perfection.

2. We must love our children for their own sakes, not merely to prove that we are good at parenting. Jesus loved us while we were yet sinners and entirely unlovable. He continues to love us even when we are unresponsive and disobedient.

3. God knows which parents to put our children with! If we entrust our mistakes to him he can turn them to good. Rotting weeds can be turned into good compost when used wisely and positively. Let's not try to justify wrong words or actions, nor

torture ourselves with remorse and guilt. If we confess our sins, he forgives and cleanses.

HOW DO YOU VIEW YOUR CHILDREN?

1. Romantically
Before we have children we can have a very romantic idea of what they will be like. Maybe we like the idea of having something small and cuddly to look after. We gaze into shops full of pretty baby clothes and imagine walking in the park with a pram (the sun, of course, is shining). In other words, we are indulging our little girl days of playing with dolls – only now the doll is alive! He or she is not accommodating and passive, to be put on one side when we've had enough of the game – he is demanding, messy, noisy and time-consuming. It is a rude awakening!

2. Resentfully
You wanted a few more years of freedom to pursue a career, but unexpectedly found yourself pregnant. Now baby has arrived, he absorbs all your time and attention. You feel out of the mainstream of life, shunted onto a side-line.

3. As a mistake
You hadn't intended to get pregnant, but you did. You sometimes (often?) wish he had never been born. You have even actually verbalised this. You feel guilty about your negative feelings, but don't know how to change.

4. As the means to your significance and identity
You've never felt significant or successful before. Now you have an infant who provides you with a label – 'mother'. You now have status and identity. But if your identity is firmly locked in to motherhood, the thought of being without children is threatening. You can either keep having children to feed your need of identity, or go to pieces when they all grow up.

5. The fulfillers of your dreams

You would love to have done more, achieved more, but realise that circumstances, choices, events changed your plans. Now you are determined that your child shall achieve and be successful and take opportunities to be 'someone'. This may seem loving, but the child can feel pressurised into pleasing Mum, and never learn to develop independently.

There are probably many other ways, good and bad, in which we can view our children. But how does God want us to see them? 'Behold, children are a gift of the Lord' (Ps 127:3, NASB).

1. God wants us to have a positive attitude to our children. We are to receive them gratefully from him. They are not mistakes, or the product of modern technology; they are entrusted to us by God.

2. With faith: Psalm 112:1–2. If we honour God, and delight in his will, God promises that our children will be 'mighty' on the earth. That means they will be strong, secure and have influence for good among their contemporaries. This promise can come into being as we lovingly train and pray for them.

DISCUSSION IDEAS

1. What made you decide to have children?

2. Did you have any ideas about what it might be like?

3. How did reality differ from your ideas?

4. Did anything about your own reactions to your children surprise you?

TRAINING WITH LOVE

1. Communication

Much of the book of Proverbs is advice from a parent to a son about fundamental issues of life. Among other things, the son is urged to prize wisdom, to speak the truth and to resist seductive flattery from unscrupulous women! He is told not to be lazy or proud, and to honour his parents, and not get drunk. In other words, the writer is very specific about what he teaches his son.

It is important that our children do not just pick up ways of thinking that are prevalent in our society. Some parents have a very passive attitude to training their children and feel it is kinder to let their children make up their own minds about ethical and moral values. On the contrary, the Bible teaches clearly that it is the parents' responsibility to communicate God's ways of living to their children.

What values should we communicate?

A clear sense of right and wrong is absolutely vital. One of the most influential and damaging views that is pervading modern thinking is a relativistic philosophy of right and wrong. It sounds very tolerant and sophisticated to deny that there are moral absolutes. It is terribly trendy to say, 'If it feels good to you, it must be right.' That is saying that it is our *feelings* that dictate morality. So if your child feels it is a good idea to hit his sister over the head with a brick, does that make it right?

It sounds very reasonable to say, 'I won't condition my child's thinking – he must have space to formulate it himself.' That is saying that he must invent his own boundaries, and it is making ignorance the deciding factor. This is actually unkind and dangerous. Would you say the same thing if he were about to run across a railway line?

It sounds kind to say, 'As long as it doesn't hurt anyone, it's all right.' That is indirectly teaching that doing the right thing is always the way that doesn't hurt. What's the point of denying yourself satisfaction if it causes you pain? It is making pain – yours or someone else's – the criterion.

There is also a lot of muddled thinking about rights. We must not deny anyone the 'right' to self-expression. In the end, that becomes, 'It doesn't matter who I hurt as long as my right to express my feelings is not repressed.' (Those 'feelings' may include anger, revenge, hatred, lust and an inflated view of my self-importance.)

Training the conscience

It is the parents' responsibility to teach a child what is right and wrong. We must be persuaded in our own minds that there is an absolute standard which we ourselves respect and practise. It is based on our belief in a loving God who has given commands for society to live by for its own good. We have lost out through woolly thinking in this area. If we attend to it, we can make our homes safer and more pleasant places, which in turn will affect our schools, streets and cities.

QUESTIONS

Imagine you discover that your five-year-old has stolen some chocolate from a shop. It was not detected at the time. Do you:
- Sigh with relief that no one else saw, and forget it?
- Congratulate him on getting away with it?
- Make a big scene, call him a 'rotten little thief' and spank him?
- Tell him quietly that stealing is never right, and help him to see that he needs to say 'sorry'?
- Anything else?

QUESTIONS

1. Your thirteen-year-old has a paper round and has to get up very early. He is very tired and decides to lie in. Does he have the right to catch up on his sleep?

2. Try to think of some other situations where your instincts may be to indulge or protect your child or to compromise, instead of sticking to principles. (See Deuteronomy 6:4, 20–25; Proverbs 22:6.)

2. Listening
Communication is two way! We need to give time to our children to hear about what they are doing at school, to listen to their thoughts and fears so that we can better understand them.

3. Physical touch
Right from the start, let us remember that the most powerful and elementary way of expressing love is by hugs, kisses, picking our children up, swinging them around, holding their hands and playing with them. It is sad but true that many young mothers don't know how to play with their children because their own parents didn't play with them. Also, many are wary of the touch factor because they were on the receiving end of unhealthy touching. But good, uncomplicated, wholesome touching and physical affection right from the start will help our children to differentiate between the good and the bad. Lots of cuddles and hugs from birth onwards helps to develop children (and later adults) who are secure and happy, and relaxed about expressing affection.

DISCUSSION IDEAS

1. Sometimes a hug is better than words. What do you think?

2. Should we expect children to kiss relatives, e.g. aunts and uncles?

3. Can kids be hugged too much? Too little?

4. How do you react when your four-year-old falls over in the street and cries?

DISCIPLINE

1. A well-disciplined child is a loved child (Heb 12:5–6). Children are like vines that will run wild if they are not pruned back. Pruning is for the good of the plant. A pruned tree has a good shape and yields good fruit. Undisciplined children have no boundaries – their lives are shapeless and undefined, and they do not realise their potential.

2. The point of discipline is mainly to teach obedience, so we do not punish children for genuine mistakes, for accidents or for ignorance; only for wilful disobedience. We must train them to obey, but we must not crush their spirits. True loving discipline does not yield fear but security.

3. Lack of discipline not only damages the child, but reflects back on the parents (Prov 10:1; 17:25; 29:15). If we are not diligent to discipline consistently and correctly we will eventually bring shame and grief upon ourselves.

4. Careful discipline will also help our children later on in life to respond positively and appreciatively to God's discipline (Heb 12:7–11).

How should we discipline?

1. With clarity
Let the child know exactly what the parameters of his freedom are.

2. With consistency
Children will try to manoeuvre you into changing your mind. Be firm!

3. By teaching responsibility
Teach them to have responsibility. For example, don't automatically pay out for everything, and don't let them assume you'll give them lifts everywhere.

4. By withholding privileges
If a child has shown lack of respect, been unkind to another child or failed to turn in homework for example, then it might be appropriate to 'ground' them – perhaps by confining them to their room for a specified period of time, or telling them they are not allowed to go out for an evening, or several evenings.

I personally preferred not to banish a child to his room on his own for more than, say, twenty minutes if he was feeling very angry and resentful. A short cooling-off period could be beneficial, but a long 'brooding' session could feed his grudges and be counter-productive. For another child, of course, longer isolation is just what he needs to calm down and reflect. You have to know your child.

5. Rewards
At one time, I found it useful to have a star system for one particular child (who was seven or eight years old) who was not

responding well to teaching on loving his little brother! I put a chart on the wall on which we stuck gold stars when he did well. A certain number of stars earned a Mars bar at the end of the week. This was fairly effective – at least, for a while.

6. Using the rod

'He who spares the rod hates his son, but he who loves him is careful to discipline him' (Prov 13:24).

'Folly is bound up in the heart of a child, but the rod of discipline will drive it far from him' (Prov 22:15).

'Do not withhold discipline from a child; if you punish him with the rod, he will not die. Punish him with the rod and save his soul from death' (Prov 23:13–14).

When used properly, a rod or wooden spoon or paddle can teach a lesson quickly and constructively, and therefore kindly.

Words are very powerful. Harsh, angry words, shouted at a cowering child in the heat of the moment, can hang in a person's mind for a lifetime, badly influencing decisions, reactions and self-image.

Careful, judicious use of a rod takes time and emotional energy; it is not something a loving parent relishes. But a momentary pain now to bring home the importance of obedience can save a lot of deeper pain in later life. If you wish to consider this issue in greater depth, please turn to Appendix 2 at the back of the book.

AFFIRMATION AND ENCOURAGEMENT

We live in a society which has largely rejected the traditional roles of mother and father. Consequently, many men and women grow without ever receiving the approval and affirmation that loving parenting should bring. A girl needs to be hugged and to be told that she is pretty by her father if she is going to learn to be natural and relaxed with the opposite sex. A boy needs to be told by both his father and mother that they think he is strong, good-looking and has great potential – or he will always be seeking approval elsewhere, and be unsure of his manliness. Keep telling your children you are proud of them. Encourage them in weak areas and praise them for strong points. Keep telling them you love them.

VISION

Let us check our ambitions for our children.

Do we want them to be obedient so that we can have a quiet life?

Do we want them to boost our egos by successfully passing exams and getting good jobs?

Do we want God to answer our prayers for them so that they avoid pain, and all have an easy life?

We can have quite selfish ambitions for our children! Instead of trying to make God fit into our plans and ideas, let us seek to find out what his plans are, and pray about how we and our children can be involved in them. God's plans are bigger than ours! He is very interested in us having a rich and happy family life for our own sakes, but he also has a bigger end in view. He wants our families to be a demonstration of his power to live in peace, love and security in a cruel and chaotic world.

Psalm 144:12 is a good prayer for our sons and daughters. Look it up. Why do you think the psalmist wants his sons and daughters to be like 'plants' and 'pillars'?

LET'S CONSIDER TRAINING

The effects of our culture

This scripture tells us to train our children, but our culture dictates that we should not influence or programme them but should let them choose their own way in life. As Christians we realise that this should not be our way, but are we influenced by this kind of thinking?

DO WE

1. Allow things to influence our children for good, e.g. Sunday school, but not positively train them at home?

2. Encourage discussion and help them to think things through?

3. Stand back when our child becomes a Christian to see if it lasts, or move in to disciple him?

4. Allow immoral behaviour on TV or in movies to go unchallenged?

It is our responsibility as parents to seek to bring biblical guidelines to shape our children's thinking and not just give in to cultural trends.

CHARACTER TRAINING

Psalm 127:3 makes it clear that children are a gift from God. As God is our Father and trains us lovingly in his ways, so we train our children. All the scriptures that teach us how to behave as Christians we seek also to instil into our children in terms of behaviour, speech and attitudes.

Training assumes relationship

Biblical training was always in the context of a deep, affectionate relationship. Consider Jesus and his disciples, Paul and Timothy. Spiritual training of our children must be built on loving relationships with them and open lines of communication.

By what means do we train?

1. By example
Do you, like me, suddenly find your heart sinks at this part? We will not be perfect examples, but if we are genuinely following Christ ourselves, this will be communicated. Our example, whatever it is, will teach our children. Let's not be afraid to face up to the challenge of being examples.

2. By teaching
All forms of instruction, both formal and informal.
   More consideration on training comes in Chapter 6.

PRAYING FOR OUR CHILDREN

'The prayer of a righteous man is powerful and effective' (Jas 5:16).

1. Be specific and be bold.

2. Ask the Lord for specific scriptures that you can use as a basis for prayer, e.g. Psalm 144:12; Psalm 112:1–2; Luke 2:52.

3. Write down prayers and record answers.

4. Remember we often pray long term; let's not be impatient. At the same time, let's be into 'now' prayers – about friendship, sickness, sports achievements, exams.

5. Be encouraged. Praying for our children will in turn affect our grandchildren and great grandchildren. There is a 'chain of truth', a baton handed on from Christian generation to Christian generation.

The following references are encouragements to prayer: Acts 2:39; Job 22:30; Isaiah 44:3; 54:13; 59:21; Psalm 103:17; Proverbs 11:21.

SPIRITUAL INPUT

1. Let the Bible become a well-known book.
• By telling them Bible stories in a form they can understand.
• By reading to older children from the Bible, and by using good picture books interspersed with their secular books.
• By acting out stories.
• By playing worship tapes – especially those made for children, e.g. Ishmael.

2. Talk about how God is answering your prayers.

3. Talk about great men and women of God, past and present.

4. Pray with them.
• Whenever an opportunity occurs, e.g. for bumps and bruises when they fall over, about friends, disappointments, facing a new challenge, fears, etc.
• On a regular basis with the rest of the family. We have always tried to have a time of Bible reading at breakfast time. Find what works for you.

5. Encourage them to worship. Explain why we raise our hands, clap and dance, and encourage them to enjoy worship.

Are you feeling breathless and overwhelmed by all these suggestions? Take heart! You don't have to do them all at once.

Leading a child to Christ

It is absolutely vital that every child has their own unique encounter with God. You may or may not be the one who leads them to Christ. A friend or youth leader could pray with them, perhaps they could go forward at a meeting or meet with God on their own anywhere, any time, at any age. We must not push them to make a commitment. Our job is to pray for it to happen and be available if necessary. Let God select the time, place, age and person involved. However, if it turns out that God gives you that privilege, you may find the following points helpful.

1. Be sure your child is ready and understands the gospel message in a simple but clear way.

2. Respond positively to any interest. Take opportunities to teach and input truth.

3. If a child is not ready, gently suggest he wait a while and disciple him until he is ready. Ask relevant questions such as: 'What is sin?' and 'Why did Jesus die on the cross?'

4. Beware of holding a child back on the basis that they're too young, or you're not sure how to handle it, when the Spirit is clearly working.

5. Lead your child in a simple prayer, preferably prayed out loud by him or her, such as, 'Lord Jesus, please forgive me for my sins and come into my life. Thank you that you loved me so much that you died on the cross for me. Help me to follow you for the rest of my life. Amen.'

6. Celebrate the experience in some way, to seal and build the memory. Encourage the child to write down his or her experience.

7. Encourage the child to tell one or two other key people about what has happened, e.g. Sunday school teacher, best friend.

8. Follow up with lots of encouragement and discipleship.

In Mark 10:14–15 Jesus said, 'Let the little children come to me, and do not hinder them, for the kingdom of God belongs to such as these. I tell you the truth, anyone who will not receive the kingdom of God like a little child will never enter it.'

As we teach our children, they will also show us something – how to receive the kingdom of God. In the dynamics of family life, there will be a constant sharing of blessing.

Remember too that we are working together with the Lord in training our children. We may sometimes feel it is a huge task, but he says to us, 'Take my yoke upon you and learn of me, for I am gentle and humble in heart and you will find rest for your souls.'

RECOMMENDED BOOKS

How to Pray for Your Children by Quin Sherrer.

Raising Children by David and Liz Holden.

Raising Kids Who Hunger for God by Benny and Sheree Phillips.

The Obedient Child by Ralph Martin.

DISCUSSION IDEAS

1. Share some helpful things that you do in your own home.

2. Where could you be a better example to your children?

3. How can you improve?

4. Choose the problems that the people in your group find relevant:

(a) Your child hits trouble at, say, school and begins to behave badly generally. At home he refuses to pray and larks about during Bible stories. What do you do?

(b) Your own spiritual life hits a bad patch. How can you guard against letting the children's discipline slip?

(c) What difficulties do you think are encountered in training the children by a Christian mother who has a non-Christian husband?

(d) What do you do if your child does not want to go to Sunday school?

(e) One of your children becomes a Christian and instantly starts nagging your other child to become a Christian, pointing out his faults and telling him that he is going to hell if he gets run over by a bus! How do you handle it?

(f) What would you suggest to parents who have just become Christians and are asking how they can begin to introduce spiritual things to their children?

Help for the Teenage Years

The period of time between thirteen and twenty years must be one of the most turbulent and complex in anyone's life. In these seven years enormous changes are accomplished physically, emotionally and mentally. You enter this phase as a child and exit as an adult.

Your teenager finds, as his body goes through hormonal and growth changes, that his emotions are like a roller-coaster. There are days when he expects to be treated as an adult, yet he still cuddles a teddy bear at night. Your daughter will be experimenting with hair dye and mascara one moment and the next she will be in jeans and short socks and roller-skates. Life is fun, exciting, yet bewildering and terrifying.

It is a time of transition and, as such, a time when feelings of insecurity, uncertainty, hopelessness and low self-esteem surface with terrifying strength. Many teenagers have enormous problems. The figures for teenage depression, suicide, pregnancy and abortion scream out their terrible message that this is a generation at odds with itself and the rest of the world.

LOOKING POSITIVELY AT THE TEENAGE YEARS

Many parents dread the teenage phase. How can we, as Christian parents, see it as not only bearable, but positive and fruitful?

1. A foundation
As a Christian I can have positive expectations of the next few years. I must be prepared for ups and downs – it will probably not be an altogether smooth ride, but it need not be disastrous.

- 'Train a child in the way he should go, and when he is old he will not turn from it' (Prov 22:6).
- 'Let us not become weary in doing good, for at the proper time we will reap a harvest if we do not give up' (Gal 6:9).

(a) If you have been sowing good seed into your children's lives already, then believe God's word that it will bear fruit. Keep watering that seed in prayer.

(b) Pray 'Thy will be done' into your child's life. The devil wants to establish his will and plans in your child, but God has a destiny for him or her. Pray it into being! God wants your child to be loved, fulfilled and at peace even more than you do.

(c) Ask God for relevant scriptures and then pray them for your children. Isaiah 49:24–25 and Psalm 128 are favourites of mine.

2. Communication

As our children grow up, we are not so immediately involved with them, and we can quickly grow apart. This means we have to work hard at making time to talk. In a busy household it is easy to fall into slipshod ways of snatching snacks and coming and going without the rest of the family being aware of the individual's movements and needs. In our house, we try to eat breakfast together and have our main evening meal together as often as possible. Sunday lunch is also an important family time for us. These meal times are frequently an opportunity for lively discussion, sharing views, or simply finding out what's going on in each other's lives.

3. Unconditional love

Teenagers need to know they are loved, no matter what. As self-awareness increases, so can lack of confidence, embarrassment at physical growth (or lack of it) and a sense of ignorance or stupidity. Everything is felt to extremes – high hopes fall into the depths of despair; a girl can suddenly feel violently jealous of her best friend even though she hates herself for it.

Exams can be failed; bedrooms become pits of nauseating untidiness; promises are broken; dreadful mistakes are made. Many teenagers at some time or other, Christians included, will find themselves sobbing in despair. 'Will I ever change? Will I ever be successful/popular/beautiful? Will I ever have a pair of Nike sport shoes, or go out with that boy/girl?'

Through it all, your children must never doubt that you love them, however difficult they are to live with. God never gave up on you, and never will. Now you are to model that unconditional love and acceptance to your children.

WHAT ABOUT CONSISTENT REBELLION?

How did God deal with us when we were rebellious to him?

1. He was unchanging (Psalm 62)

God is a rock. Parents must be rocks, firm and consistent, not diluting their standards. Though our teenagers may kick against our authority, they still need it, and will be insecure without it.

Set standards; agree on times to be in. Let them know your expectations of their behaviour. Obviously the reins will not be as tight as when they were little. A lot of skill is involved in letting out the rope – we will make mistakes and sometimes allow too much freedom or not enough. However, aim at making clear, reasonable decisions, so that they know where the lines are drawn. There will be times when it is right to change in detail, but not in principle or attitude.

2. He waited for our return (Luke 15)

Eventually the father of the prodigal son had to let him go and find out his folly the hard way. Many parents know the agony of seeing their teenage son or daughter in a 'far country'.

The father never gave up watching and waiting for the prodigal's return. Keep praying for it, expecting it – and be there for them when it happens!

3. He showed patience (Psalm 103:6–14)

God is slow to anger, abounding in mercy. Patience is often something that parents of teens are short on. But how patient God has been with us! He knows our frame; he understands our vulnerable, weak spots; he knows the pace we can cope with. David said, 'Thy gentleness makes me great' (Ps 18:35, NASB).

Now let's extend this to our teenagers. We often attribute to them more maturity than they have yet reached, and then we are disappointed when they display immaturity. Remember, they still carry many childish feelings and concepts in what may be a well-developed body.

4. He had hope
God never abandoned his plans and destiny for us. He just kept on working away at us, conforming us to his image. God has plans for your children.

Look up Psalms 102:28; 112:1–2; 127:3,5; 144:12.

He is full of hope and expectation for our children. Ask the Holy Spirit to fill you with that same hope and the faith to pray it into reality.

Remember also that we are to pray for God's plans to be established in them, not our own desires and ambitions.

WHAT WE NEED TO KNOW ABOUT TEENS

We have already said that teens need our unconditional love, patience, prayers, communication and hope. They also need:

1. Adequate rest
They don't think they do, but they do! They think they can get away with endless late nights, but as we all know eventually they become weary, irritable and weepy – even more than usual. Try to insist on a reasonable amount of sleep.

2. Space
When they were little, they did everything openly – feeding, playing and dressing, and (in my experience) shared bedrooms, even beds! Then with the advent of teenage years, they begin to want to be on their own. They need privacy, time to themselves and if they can have their own bedrooms, so much the better. Respect their privacy.

3. Goals

Teenagers are not generally good at time-keeping. They need help in structuring programmes to get homework done on time and avoid the inevitable panic of the last-minute rush. I am grateful for the help that some of my children have had from teachers in setting goals and learning the discipline of working steadily to achieve them.

They also need something ahead to focus on, so that they can develop a sense of progress, rather than a vague, nebulous lifestyle which leads to confusion. However, they also need time to just 'hang-out' with friends occasionally.

4. Challenges

Youth responds to challenge. Don't let's be over-protective of our teens. When your church is engaged in evangelism, involve the youth. Encourage them to take risks in praying for the sick, arranging evangelistic outreaches and concerts, and open-air preaching.

5. The baptism of the Spirit

The sooner the better. Make room for them; encourage them to use the gifts of the Spirit too. Often teenagers flourish when they are baptised in the Spirit and led by enthusiastic young leaders are let loose in schools and streets in evangelistic outreaches. (See Appendix 1 for a fuller discussion.)

6. The grace of God

We often preach grace to the main body of the church, but keep our teens condemned with heavy doses of law, saying, 'Don't do this/go there/wear this.' They need exactly the same motivation as the rest of us: the unconditional love of God which saves us and goes on working in us, producing love and gratitude which make us want to please him.

7. Christian friends

These can be an invaluable strength. All my children benefit greatly from the comfort and godly protection that Christian friendships generate. Pray for them to find Christian friends if they don't have any yet.

8. Somewhere to meet with friends

A well-run youth club can be a great blessing if you are lucky enough to have people with the gifting, dedication and energy to lead it. Such clubs need to be imaginative, creative and relevant to modern children; able to address and understand current issues without buying into wrong worldly values. Tricky. I am full of admiration and gratitude for the young people in my church who run excellent clubs and have befriended and helped my children at crucial stages of their lives.

A FINAL THOUGHT

God called many great men and women in their teens, including the following:

David	(1 Sam 16)	C.H. Spurgeon
Daniel	(Dan 1)	George Whitefield
Jeremiah	(Jer 1)	Mahesh Chavda
Esther	(Esther 1)	Many missionaries,
Timothy	(1 Tim 1)	historic & contemporary
Mary	(Lk 1)	men and women.

Encourage your teenagers to develop their personal walk with God:

- By reading good Christian biographies and devotional books.
- By praying with as well as for them.

Recommended Reading

Campbell, Ross. *How to Really Love Your Child.* SP Trust

Dobson, James. *Hide and Seek.* Hodder

Dobson, James. *Parenting isn't for Cowards.* Word UK

Holden, David & Liz, *Raising Children — a Parents Privilege.* Kingsway Publications

Hubbard, Richard. *Taking Children Seriously.* Marshall Pickering

White, Rob & Marian. *My Family, My Church.* Kingsway Publications

Chapter 4

Self-control

Part One:
The New Self, Controlled by Truth

The New Testament writers quite frequently exhort their readers to cultivate *self-control*. It might surprise you how often it is mentioned.

Who else does Paul say should be self-controlled?

LOOK UP

Titus 1:8; 2:6; 1 Timothy 3:2.

Paul also tells us that one of the marks of ungodly people is lack of self-control (2 Tim 3:2–3).

QUESTION

In Acts 24 Felix discussed certain things with Paul, and 'was afraid'. What were these things?

WHAT IS SELF-CONTROL?

It is the ability to say 'no', to be in command of one's appetites and desires. It is to be able to rule desires and passions; to govern one's impulses and actions; to make right choices and not be under compulsion.

We live in an existentialist age, where denying oneself is looked upon as dreary, old-fashioned, 'puritanical' and repressive. If it feels good, do it! Live for the moment! Enjoy now and blow the consequences! Let it all hang out! Don't bottle it up! These are common phrases, along with words like 'binge', 'blow-out', 'freak-out'. Self-restraint is no longer admired as a virtue.

But, as Christians, we have been called to live lives that are based on an entirely different foundation; that is, not to be self-pleasers, but God-pleasers. We are not to be abandoned to self-gratification, but self-controlled.

LOOK UP

2 Peter 1:6. What comes before self-control? What comes as a result of it? What 'knowledge' do we need to base self-control on?

OUR 'BC' DAYS

LOOK UP

Ephesians 2:1–5.

---

1. Our 'BC' Life

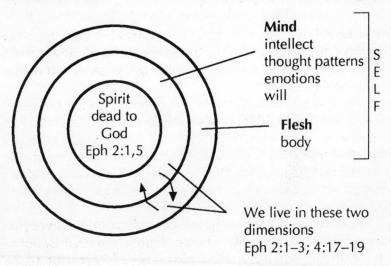

Mind
intellect
thought patterns
emotions
will

S
E
L
F

Flesh
body

Spirit
dead to
God
Eph 2:1,5

We live in these two
dimensions
Eph 2:1–3; 4:17–19

2. Our Born Again Life

Mind and flesh (self) no
longer govern us but
must be brought under
the control of the Spirit.

Eph 4:22–23
Rom 12:1–2
2 Cor 10:4–5
Rom 8

A 'new heart'
Spirit alive to
God
Eph 2:5

Before we were born again, our spirits were dead to God. We
lived on two levels, our 'minds' and our 'flesh' (v.3). (See
diagram.)

Our minds include our thought patterns, emotions and wills.
Our flesh is our bodies and bodily appetites for food, sex and rest.

Together, our minds and bodies constitute our 'self', and before we became Christians we lived to please our 'self' (Eph 2:3; 4:18–21).

ALIVE TO GOD (EPHESIANS 2:4–5)

When we were born again our spirits came alive. We were given a 'new heart' which responds to the love of God. We began to hear his voice, and talk with him. At that time we said something like, 'Come and take over my life, Lord Jesus.'

We have now come under new management. We have a new spirit that desires to please Jesus. So from now on, our minds and bodies have to be brought under his control. Paul says that we have to stop living in the old ways and start renewing our minds (Eph 4:23; Rom 12:1–2).

Our *spirits* are new and will never die.

Our *minds* start a process of being renewed as we learn to bring them under the control of the Holy Spirit.

Our *bodies* will never be made new because they are subject to age and decay, but we will get new ones in heaven (Rom 8:12–25; 2 Cor 4:16). Meanwhile, however, the enemy uses its appetites, which are not wrong in themselves, to undermine and fight against what the Spirit is doing in us.

Living for Jesus means that we bring the self – that is, the mind and the flesh – under his control. We do this by:

1. *Letting his truth change our minds.* As we receive truth and apply it, it affects the way we think, our attitudes, our decisions. We learn to rule our emotions and our speech.

2. *Subduing and ruling our flesh.* Paul uses strong expressions for this. He says, 'I beat my body' (1 Cor 9:27); 'Put to death, therefore, whatever belongs to your earthly nature' (Col 3:5).

All that we have described so far is called *sanctification* – the process of becoming holy. In 1 Peter 1:15–16 we read that God calls us to be holy because he is holy. As we become more like him, the fruit of the Spirit begins to show in our lives.

LOOK UP

Galatians 5:16–26 and consider the following questions:

1. If you are walking in the Spirit, what will you not do (v.16)?

2. What are the deeds of the flesh (vv.19–21)?

3. What is the fruit of the Spirit?

Notice that self-control is on the list. The self-control that we are talking about is the result of a life submitted to the Spirit, where God reigns.

PRACTICAL OUTWORKING

We have seen that self-control for a Christian is far deeper than telling oneself, 'I must try harder,' or, 'I will not eat sweets,' or (as some think), 'I must not express my emotions, or do things I like doing.'

We have a *purpose* for self-control: to be holy.

We have a *foundation* for self-control: a born-again spirit.

We have the *keys* for self-control: renewing the mind and saying 'no' to the flesh.

Now what does this mean on a day-to-day level for me as a Christian woman?

Remember we have an enemy who wants to rob us. He works by attacking us through our mind and flesh. He wants us to be permanently in *disarray, discontent, despondency* and *condemnation.* God intends us to be at peace with him and with ourselves.

TEMPTATION THROUGH THE MIND AND EMOTIONS

1. Disarray
This is often the result of a cluttered and confused state of mind. Is my life disordered? Do I live in squalor, clutter and untidiness? Do I put off chores because I'm lazy or bored? Or because I'm tired? If I'm tired, is it because I am undisciplined about bedtimes?

2. Discontent
Am I constantly wishing I had a nicer house or garden, better clothes or a particular car? Do I wish I had more children/fewer children/no children? Do I wish I were thinner or fitter?

3. Despondency
Do I live in a negative mentality: How will I ever cope with too little money/ a sickness/ my mother/ my in-laws? It's raining/too hot/too cold. We'll never afford a holiday/school uniforms/a new washing machine!

4. Condemnation
I'm a hopeless mother; a bad witness. I shouldn't be so cross with the kids. I shouldn't be so overweight. I'm always making mistakes.

See how the enemy attacks our minds with these weapons. If we give in to them we become immobilised, passive, negative.

Self-control is to do with refusing these things, girding up our minds and taking action. 'Gird your minds for action' (1 Pet 1:13, NASB).

How do we do this? The verse goes on, 'Keep sober.' Think about this. It isn't necessarily to do with drinking – more to do with, 'Think carefully, consider, weigh up the factors involved.'

What are we to think about? The verse goes on, 'Set your hope fully on the grace of the Lord Jesus.' That's the key. We overcome the attacks on our minds by considering him and what he has done for us. We can't hope to be perfect, but the good news is that we don't have to be, because he is perfect for us.

Remember, we learn to renew our minds and change our behaviour by letting truth control us.

Part Two: Action Stations!

You have probably noticed that 'self-control' is variously translated in different versions as 'sensible', 'discreet', 'chaste' and 'pure'. These words are really amplifying the whole idea of self-control, and they help us with the practical outworking of it.

In Part One of this section, we talked about how a Christian no longer lives being dictated to by his mind and body, but how his spirit is now alive, receiving truth from God which changes his thinking and behaviour. Now we need to consider:

USE OF OUR BODIES

Made by God

As we have already seen, our bodies are not evil. In fact they are 'wonderfully made' (Ps 139:13–16). God put us together lovingly and carefully, and gave us an amazing capacity to move, run, dance, sing, eat, drink, make love and generally enjoy life. These things are normal and right. But we must rule them, not let them rule us. Our enemy attacks us by getting at us through our physical appetites, tempting us to use our bodies sinfully (1 Cor 6:12–20).

Temples

Paul says that our bodies are 'temples of the Holy Spirit'. God must like them if he wants to live in them. So he wants us to look after them well and treat them with respect. The things we do in them must be consistent with who they belong to.

Temple maintenance

1. We may need to review how we treat our bodies. Perhaps we are abusing them by eating too much, drinking too much, or not taking enough exercise.

2. Maybe we need to think through the implications of a wrong sexual relationship. A Christian woman must not indulge in sex before marriage, or outside her marriage relationship. We are told quite clearly that we must rid ourselves of such things (Col 3:5–7).

How do we 'clean up'?

In 1 John 1:7–9 we read that we must confess wrong actions and ask God to forgive us and cleanse us. Self-control is about 'fleeing' from those things that hinder our spiritual growth, such as sexual immorality, greed, indiscipline, etc.

LOOK UP

1 Corinthians 6:12–20.

This passage shows us that we are not to live as though we are just one big bundle of appetites that must be gratified. Our bodies are temporary dwellings and we will eventually do without them But in the meantime, let's use them well to honour God.

QUESTIONS

Study 1 Corinthians 6:12–20 again.

1. **How does this affect a Christian's approach to eating/drinking/smoking?**

2. **What does it mean to be 'mastered' by anything?**

3. **Why is immorality so serious for a Christian?**

4. **Who is affected by immoral behaviour?**

5. **Why does it grieve the Holy Spirit?**

6. **How can we honour God with our bodies?**

USE OF OUR TIME

'Whatever you do, work at it with all your heart, as working for the Lord, not for men, since you know that you will receive an inheritance from the Lord as a reward. It is the Lord Christ you are serving' (Col 3:23–24). These words help to establish that as Christian women it is not what we do but the attitude and motivation with which we do it that are important to God.

If you are a young mum with a new baby, you may well find yourself at home for quite long periods of time. Perhaps up to now you have been used to running a busy office or being in charge of a hospital ward or a classroom full of turbulent kids. Being a housewife will be an absolute doddle! Your house will be a model of style and cleanliness and the baby a total delight, chuckling contentedly in the shiny new buggy or pram. You can do it with one hand tied behind your back!

A few weeks (days?) later, the house is a squalid dump, the baby never stops screaming or spouting nasty sludge from both ends, and you are so tired you can barely stand up. What happened to the dream?

Be realistic!
Being a housewife is a devalued occupation. The assumption is that it's a job for fools who can't find anything better to do. Actually the truth is that it requires skill and determination to juggle successfully the things that have to be done. These include being a cook and dietician, decorator, nurse, teacher, cleaner, financier, needleworker, gardener, etc. Most of us are only good at some of these things and the rest we learn slowly.

Give yourself time!
Adjusting to a new baby is very demanding. Your hormones take time to settle down, you are probably not getting enough sleep and your body has not yet regained its pre-birth contours. So you feel depressed.

Give yourself mercy!
Establish a routine. If you were a student you lived with a timetable; if you were in an office there was probably a structure to your day. If you are mostly at home now you may find it surprisingly difficult to be responsible for your time. If you let events dictate your day, you may fall into drifting; then at the end of the day you can feel frustrated at how little seems to have been achieved. On the other hand, you may find you are rushing from one thing to another without a clear goal, and you are getting overtired and confused.

The two traps are passivity and over-activity
A lot depends on the stage of family life. If you have a new baby, just getting a meal on the table is a triumph. Anything else is a bonus.

But when you have had several children and the youngest is at school, your expectations will be very different (we hope!).

TAKE ACTION

1. Make a list of things that need to be done, for example, washing, ironing, shopping, cooking, vacuuming, meeting children from school, helping with homework, changing sheets on beds, etc.

2. Decide which things on your list have to be done today (be realistic).

3. Decide what days you will shop, clean, meet friends.

4. Each day list what you intend to do, including phone calls, letters and meetings. Cross them off as you do them. It is very satisfying to see rows of crossed-off items at the end of the day.

No doubt you will devise your own methods. But being in (reasonable) control of your time helps you to feel 'on top' and guards you against frustration and confusion.

USE OF OUR MONEY

Remember we are talking about self-control. That means our 'self' coming under God's control so that we operate under an entirely new principle: all that I have has been entrusted to me by God. How can I handle it so as to honour him?

With thankfulness
Instead of being discontented because of what you don't have, make the best use of what you do have.

With efficiency
Work out your priorities – with your husband, if you have one. If you are on your own, maybe a friend can help you if you need help.

MORE ACTION

1. **Work out your main outgoings – utility bills, mortgage, car tax, petrol, etc. – not forgetting giving.**

2. **Agree on an amount for housekeeping. Different people will have different systems, but stick to some basic principles. Here are some fairly obvious ones:**
   - **Buy basic necessities first.**
   - **Be ruthless (do you really need that Mars bar?).**
   - **Avoid impulse buying.**
   - **Swap ideas for cheap recipes.**
   - **Use charity shops for bargain clothes, swap outgrown children's clothes with friends.**
   - **Look for people who are good at managing and learn from them.**

Without fear
God has promised to supply our needs. As we give to him, he has promised to give back to us (Phil 4:18–19; Mt 6:31–34; Lk 6:38).

Recommended Reading

Nee Watchman. *The Normal Christian Life*. Kingsway Publications

Holden, David. *Battle for the Mind*. Kingsway Publications

Sherman, Dean. *Spiritual Warfare*. YWAM

Chapter 5

Being Homemakers

1. At the fireside (John 21:1–11)

The disciples had been out fishing all night with no success. They had also been through some deeply traumatic events. They were tired, cold, hungry and discouraged.

Then Jesus came and changed everything. What did he do?

At that fireside he created a context of simple, tender caring. The disciples were fed, affirmed, instructed and encouraged.

2. Another fireside (John 18:18, 25–26)

This fireside was not lit by Jesus. The people around it were strangers. Here there was no comfort or acceptance for Peter; he felt threatened and vulnerable, fearful and defensive. In his insecurity, he lied and swore.

3. Whose fire (Isaiah 50:10–11)?

'See here, you who live in your own light, and warm yourselves from your own fires and not from God's, you will live among sorrows' (Living Bible).

A traditional picture of a home is of a family grouped cosily around a fireside. The curtains are drawn against a dark, maybe stormy night. The family are close together, the firelight flickering on their faces. They hold steaming cups of soup or cocoa, and some are holding out slices of bread on toasting forks to the fire. Let your imagination run and add some more details!

What do you think this conveys? Add your suggestions to the following list: belonging, safety, warmth, acceptance.

The human spirit craves these elements of love and acceptance, security, significance, identity. God intended the family to be a context where they could be nurtured and developed. God wants to demonstrate his love through human relationships.

LOOK UP

Ephesians 3:14–15. What do these verses tell us about

1. God?

2. his relationship to us?

3. the origin of 'family'?

In fact, all human relationships have their origin in God.

Fatherhood: 1 John 3:1, Matthew 6:32.
Motherhood: Matthew 23:37; Isaiah 49:15.
Brotherhood: John 20:17; Hebrews 2:11.
Sonship: Hebrews 2:11; Luke 3:22.

A family where God lights the fire has all the potential for sparking off flames of his love, light and power in each individual (Eph 3:16).

LOOK UP

Psalm 128.

1. What is the man like who fears God (vv.1–2)?

2. What is his wife like?

3. What can he expect for his children?

A family where God has not lit the fire may be good, but not the best. The people in it are trying to warm themselves from their own fires; there may be rich colours and beautiful furnishings, but the foundation of the home is human philosophy and endeavour. Isaiah prophesies eventual disappointment and sorrow.

LOOK UP

Psalm 127:1–2. Is the Lord the foundation and inspiration of your home?

THE HOMEMAKER

The wife and mother is central to the home. She is the one who has most influence on the atmosphere, the colours, the fabrics. She usually decides the menu and, to a large extent, what everyone wears. She is indispensable, the pivotal point. She has power to create an atmosphere in which everyone is either happy and relaxed, or uncomfortable and tense. Do you think this is true? Perhaps we sometimes underestimate our importance!

PROVERBS 31

Here is a vivid, detailed picture of the ideal homemaker. It is so detailed that many think it is modelled on a real woman known to the author, but I think it is more likely to be an amalgam based on several.

A look at her could be a bit intimidating. She was so incredibly energetic, industrious, creative and wise that she seems to present an impossibly high standard! However, I am sure we are not meant to copy her slavishly, but rather pick up some principles.

WHAT MAKES A GOOD HOMEMAKER?

1. Trusting relationships

At the heart of a good home must be a good marriage relationship (unless of course you are a single parent). This woman's life was motivated by wanting to bring good to her husband and not harm. Consequently, he trusted her and gave her plenty of scope. If husband and wife are not living in mutual love and respect, the home will be a place of discord and tension. Children are quick to sense a strained atmosphere, and this will make them feel anxious, insecure and frightened.

2. Hard work

This woman was not afraid of hard work, and neither should we be. Homemakers are often dismissed as women 'sitting around at home vegetating'. You are probably thinking, 'Chance would be a fine thing!'

Certainly a lot of drudgery has been removed with the invention of washing machines, dishwashers, microwave ovens, etc. But running a home, especially if there are several young children, is undeniably hard work. Trawling round a supermarket with a wayward trolley and one or two even more wayward children can be exhausting. So can piles of ironing, cleaning bathrooms, digging the garden, and making beds, to say nothing of broken nights and frantic meal times.

So are you condemned to life on a treadmill? It depends on your attitude.

REMEMBER

1. **You can choose.** The reality is that running a home and raising a family is hard work. Face it squarely. The next 5, 10, 15 or 20 years (depending on the size of your family) could be absolutely deadly, with you resenting every moment in your self-made prison, if you choose to be negative. Or they could be some of the happiest, richest, most fulfilling years of your life, if you choose to be positive.

2. **A home is never static.** You won't always be breast-feeding, potty-training or smacking bottoms – although it sometimes feels like it. (You could however be making shepherd's pie and picking up dirty socks for many years to come!) Life goes in phases. Enjoy and endure!

3. **Homemaking has unique rewards:**
   - A newly bathed child, pink and warm.
   - The smell of freshly baked cakes.
   - Time to go for a walk.
   - A pile of laundry freshly ironed.
   - A happy child sticky with jam, as he 'helps' you cook jam tarts.
   - The feel of smooth clean sheets as you slide into bed at the end of a long day.

   Make your own list. You'll be surprised at the many things you have to be thankful for!

3. Creativity

This woman enjoyed weaving, spinning and sewing. You may prefer painting and decorating, icing cakes, or making birthday cards. Perhaps you are good at making jam or bread, or arranging flowers, or making jewellery. Or perhaps you run your own business.

Whatever your preference, don't suppress it! It's all right spending time being creative (God does). We can become so busy with bare necessities that creative impulses get buried.

It is a delight to go into a home and find unique touches – even if it is only smudgy paintings by a toddler, or a candle on the dinner table. Colourful cushions, photographs well placed and pretty pieces of china need not be expensive, but they add colour to memories and help create an atmosphere of care and thoughtfulness.

4. Ingenuity

Not all of us are entrepreneurs like this woman was. She saw all sorts of possibilities, such as buying a field, planting it and using the profit to create a vineyard. She also had a cottage industry going – she made and sold garments and belts. I have a friend who hand-rears calves for beef.

We may not have the flair or the resources for such ventures, but we can find ways of making the money stretch. We can hunt for bargains or find ways of making things. (There are women in my church who have made their own furniture, as well as curtains, clothes and pictures.) Let's learn from each other.

5. Discipline

Our Proverbs 31 lady is self-disciplined. She gets up early; she thinks ahead; she delegates wisely. Her body is in good shape (v.17), she does not waste time (v.27) and she is a good example to her family (v.28).

By her disciplined, fulfilled life, focused on fearing God and blessing her husband, she earns the love and respect of her family.

6. Kindness
She is not only formidably efficient and industrious, she is kind-hearted and open-handed. In Titus 2, Paul particularly mentions kindness as a quality that he wants us to cultivate, so we will devote a whole section to this subject (Chapter 7).

7. Dignity and self-esteem
She is not so buried under domestic detail that she neglects herself. She is like a queen, calm and poised. She spends time on her appearance (v.22). She is at peace with herself, so that there is an aura of serenity about her (v.25).

8. The secret
She fears God. Therefore she pursues excellence (not perfection), and her life is fruitful and glorifies God.

Recommended Reading
Schaeffer, Edith. *Hidden Art.* Crossway
Schaeffer, Edith. *What is a Family?* Highland

Chapter 6

What is a home?

We have already seen that 'family' is a concept that came out of the heart of God. It is not a biological or sociological accident. God invented it for our good and for his glory. Something of himself is embodied in every family. Strongly linked with family is the place where family is rooted and expresses itself: home.

I. A PLACE OF REFUGE

Safety, shelter, protection – these words are appropriate to the 'nest', the context in which vulnerable, defenceless young are born, nurtured and raised.

LOOK UP

Deuteronomy 32:11. The mother eagle is seen caring for her young – feeding them and training them to maturity.

LOOK UP

1. **Deuteronomy 33:27. As the mother eagle swoops under the chicks, catching them as they fall, so God is like a safe refuge, spreading his arms beneath us, always stable, always there.**

How tragic that in today's society, the place where children should be most safe and protected is often the place where they are most damaged.

2. **Psalms 71:5; 90:1–2; 91:1–4. Discuss the ways in which God models 'home' to us.**

---

2. A PLACE OF TRAINING

'Train a child in the way he should go, and when he is old he will not turn from it' (Prov 22:6). This is true whether the training is positive or negative. It has a lasting effect, so let it be our ambition to train wisely and diligently.

It is alarming to think that the way we behave, speak to and relate to our children has a direct bearing on how they see themselves, others and life itself. Often we are unconsciously instilling good and bad patterns of thinking into them. What we don't do or say can be as significant to them as what we do say or do.

QUESTIONS

1. **What things did your mother or father say to you that coloured your attitude to, for example, money, work, illness, Christmas, reading, dogs or anything else?**

2. **What did they say to you about each other?**

3. **What did they say about you (e.g. you were pretty or plain, a nuisance, stupid, lovable, etc.)?**

Obviously the home is a place of training for:

Acceptable behaviour

This includes potty training, using a knife and fork, eating foods that are nutritious but not necessarily liked, not indulging in temper tantrums, doing up shoe laces, and general courtesy.

We don't teach acceptable behaviour because we want our children to be constricted into strait-jacket regimens, but because we know their paths in life will be much smoother as they master basic skills.

Relating

If we train our children to respect and obey Mummy and Daddy, teacher, youth leaders, etc., they will find it easier to respect and relate to employers, managers, rules of sport and the laws of the land later on. Anarchy in the home must spread to anarchy outside and the general disruption of society.

Attitudes and ambitions

What ambitions do we have for our children? That they become famous? Rich? Academically brilliant? Or simply that they marry a nice boy or girl and live around the corner so that we can enjoy the grandchildren?

These ambitions may be natural and not wrong in themselves. But if they are not in line with God's plans they will become stumbling-blocks, making it difficult for them to find and pursue God's will.

DISCUSSION IDEAS

1. **What sort of things should we desire for our children (see Psalm 144:12)?**

2. **Why is it desirable for young men to be 'like well-nurtured plants'? And for young women to be 'like pillars'?**

3. **What do they see inspiring us? What ambitions motivate us? Do we have any?**

---

3. A PLACE OF MEMORIES

The home is a place where we look back as well as forward. Good memories are a powerful cement for bonding a family together. As they grow older, the family members derive great delight from retelling stories that have become woven into the fabric of family life. Like the following example:

'Do you remember when we went on that long walk one Christmas and Joel fell into a huge puddle?'

'Oh yes. We were dragging the sledge along. It wasn't snowy, but we had to take it out because it was new. We slid down in mud instead!'

'Was I born then, Mummy?'

'No, darling, but I remember so clearly when you were born – it was snowing then!'

Groans – Mum needs no encouragement to remember the births of all five babies! Although they pretend they don't want to hear it again, they are all glad that each birth was such a precious, special event.

Such memories not only create warm pleasant feelings, they nurture a sense of being rooted, of belonging, of having foundations. *Deliberately plan family times and work at creating memories.*

Bad memories

These can produce pain, fear, low self-esteem and feelings of rejection, bitterness and anger. They affect the way we relate to the world around us. We learn to react defensively, or aggressively, or fearfully in order to protect ourselves from further pain.

BE RENEWED

Read Psalm 139 and use the last verse as a prayer. Let the Holy Spirit expose wrong ways of thinking. Then you can confess them and ask him to help you pull down those 'strongholds' of thinking, and renew your mind by applying truth.

QUESTIONS

1. Can you recall some happy memories? What feelings do they produce?

2. Can you recall any very unpleasant memories? Do they disturb you? Are you allowing them to affect your attitudes to yourself or anyone else?

3. Are you grateful for your childhood, or sad and bitter about it? Are you willing to ask God for help and healing?

4. How can you cultivate good memories in your own family?

HANDING ON THE BATON

Israel had a unique history, being a nation delivered from slavery, led through the wilderness for forty years where their needs were miraculously provided for, and then proceeding to enter and possess the promised land.

Moses was anxious that this history should be preserved, and that each individual would feel deeply rooted in this rich heritage. So the parents were given the responsibility of teaching it to their children. The incredible interventions of God down through the years were to be repeated from generation to generation.

QUESTION

Look up Deuteronomy 6:20–25. What blessings would come from this (vv.24–25)?

There are principles here that are important for us. To know God's ways, and to live in them, was for their own good. In fact their survival depended on it.

We live in a nation where God's ways are no longer taught diligently, broadly speaking. Our society is becoming increasingly fragmented, as the foundations are being eroded. Strong Christian families that live by God's word can be an important uniting factor, and can have far-reaching influence. Let's be diligent in teaching God's ways in our homes, and becoming part of a chain of truth.

Recommended Reading

Mains Burton, Karen. Open Heart, Open Home. Nova Publishing

Chapter 7

Kindness

I had never thought seriously about this word before doing this study. It is the sort of everyday word we take for granted. We say that 'the weather was kind', or 'someone did a kind deed'.

QUESTIONS

1. Can you think of some people you would describe as kind?

2. What other words would you use to describe their actions?

3. What do you feel like when they are kind to you?

Maybe some of the words you used to describe kindness included gentle, patient, generous, thoughtful, friendly. Kindness is not usually displayed in great heroism, drama and courage. It is, rather, a word with a softer, milder feel and embraces actions which are thoughtful and warm. They may even be unnecessary, but they smooth the rough edges of our ways.

KIND ACTIONS

Think of some 'kind' actions, e.g. baking a cake for a pressured friend, tenderly wiping a child's grazed knee and 'kissing it better', or checking on an elderly neighbour who lives alone.

Obviously there are endless ways in which we could show kindness, but is it only about doing good deeds? There are plenty of non-Christian people who do that all the time.

QUESTION

In what ways should Christian women excel in kindness?

ATTITUDE OF HEART

LOOK UP

Galatians 5:22. One fruit of the Spirit is 'kindness'. So it springs from an inner life of walking with God. As we get closer to him we start to show his characteristics.

If you have been on the receiving end of 'duty kindness', a seemingly kind act done grudgingly, or to save face, or to make the person look good, you know how empty it feels. Kindness motivated by the love of God is quite different. It is encouraging and makes you feel loved.

QUESTION

Philippians 2:1–5. The attitude of heart that we are talking about is set out for us in verse 3: 'Do nothing out of selfish ambition or vain conceit, but in humility consider others better than yourselves.'

What are the key words here?

Kindness is rooted in unselfishness which is always looking for ways to help and bless others (v.4). Verse 5 tells us that this was the attitude that Jesus had. Let's see how he showed kindness in his life.

JESUS WAS KIND

1. He healed people. He saw them in their suffering and distress, and healed them. We might long for this gift, but take note that it was no picnic! It involved long hours, fatigue, pressure from crowds, touching lepers, being touched by those thought to be unclean, interruptions, inconvenience, no time even to eat. It also incurred disapproval and hostility at times. Healing is wonderful, but it is also costly.

2. He socialised with the socially unacceptable (see Luke 7:34, 39). He was willing to be of no reputation.

3. He served others (Mk 10:45). He washed the disciples' feet (Jn 13), he fed the five thousand (Lk 9) and he provided breakfast on the beach (Jn 21).

4. He was approachable. Children felt at home with him; so did Zacchaeus the tax man, Nicodemus the Pharisee, the Centurion at Capernaum, Simon the fisherman, Mary Magdalene the forgiven prostitute and Joanna the wife of Herod's steward. He was accessible to people from all walks of life, and was called the 'friend of tax collectors and sinners' (Lk 7:34).

5. He answered their questions and taught them (Mk 6:34). Jesus had great compassion for the people because they were like sheep without a shepherd. So he gave himself to teaching them. In Luke 10 a lawyer asked a question. Jesus didn't give a quick answer, but told a wonderful parable, 'The Good Samaritan', which so clearly shows the kindness and mercy of God.

GOD IS KIND

1. Everything Jesus did was to show us what God is like.

> ### LOOK UP
>
> John 1:18 and John 14:6 –9. These are important verses that tell us that if we want to know what God is like, then we must look at Jesus.

We have seen that kindness is linked with compassion, unselfishness, gentleness, friendliness, generosity and love, and that Jesus displayed all of these things. God is kind.

2. God's kindness is also seen in his patience with us.

LOOK UP

Romans 2:4. He gives us time to come to repentance. He is not quick to judge or condemn. He is longing for us to respond to him, so that we can more fully appreciate his riches and his love. Repentance means to change direction. He gives us time to change.

3. Peter speaks of our salvation as 'the kindness of the Lord'.

LOOK UP

1 Peter 2:3 (NASB). This kindness is personified in Jesus: 'The kindness and love of God our Saviour appeared' (Titus 3:4). God showed his kindness to us in giving Jesus to us – an act of supreme generosity and self-giving. Love is kind (1 Cor 13:4).

KINDNESS AND FORGIVENESS (EPHESIANS 4:32)

This is a very important aspect of kindness, and one that only Christians can really understand and act upon. We can only really forgive when we have received God's forgiveness. When we come to the cross and see that Jesus was there to pay our debt; when we see it was our selfishness and sin that put him there; when we humble ourselves and ask for his forgiveness, we see everything in a different light. How can we refuse then to forgive those who have sinned against us?

QUESTIONS

Study the parable in Matthew 18:23–25. Ask yourself:

1. Am I holding bitterness and anger in my heart against anyone?

2. What does this do to my relationship with God (Eph 4:30)?

3. What must I do (Eph 4:31)?

You have a choice! You can hold on to your bitterness (believing you are justified in this – see 1 John 1:8), or you can put it away.

Ephesians 4:32 exhorts us to be kind and forgive, because God has forgiven us. Be kind to others and forgive. Be kind to yourself and forgive.

Your peace with God will be restored when you confess your bitterness, receive forgiveness, and then forgive the one who wronged you.

Recap
So far we have seen that kindness starts with a heart attitude of humility and unselfishness, exemplified by Jesus, who 'went around doing good' (Acts 10:38) and showed us how to forgive. Kindness can only be understood in action. Although it is rooted in an attitude of heart, it has its outworking in very practical ways.

KIND WOMEN

The woman in Proverbs 31

This busy, creative, adventurous woman was also kind. She provided well for her household but also gave to the poor. She was generous and open-hearted. (See also Proverbs 21:13 and 1 John 3:17.)

Tabitha (Acts 9:36)

She abounded in deeds of kindness. What were they? She made clothes for the people in her church! Her death caused a major crisis. The saints were so distressed, they sent for Peter who raised her from the dead. She wasn't a leader – just a lady who was kind and served. This might elevate our whole understanding of the importance of kind deeds.

HOSPITALITY

This was a major feature of the early church (Acts 2:46; 4:32). The people did not cling possessively to their homes; they were open-hearted and gladly shared their homes and possessions with one another.

Paul was often on the receiving end of hospitality when he travelled. He often sent greetings to households (2 Tim 4:19; Col 4:15; 1 Cor 16:15). Often churches would meet in these houses. At least two belonged to women: Nympha in Colossae, and Lydia in Philippi (Acts 16:15), and they showed Paul kindness by inviting him to stay.

We are not only to show hospitality to Christians, but also to strangers (Heb 13:2). Sometimes these turn out to be angels! (See also Romans 12:13 and 1 Peter 4:9.)

QUESTIONS

1. What is the difference between entertaining and hospitality?

2. What are we offering when we offer hospitality (e.g. a genuine welcome, 'duty', trying to impress, etc.)?

3. Who should we offer hospitality to (Rom 12:13; Heb 13:2; Mt 25:34–40)?

4. What excuses do we give not to offer hospitality? Which of these are valid?

5. Is it a good thing to allow our guests to serve us, e.g. by doing the washing up? Why?

6. What makes a home welcoming to a guest (adult or child)?

7. What types of hospitality can we offer? Any creative ideas?

MATTHEW 25:31–40

Jesus taught us that acts of kindness not only bring blessing to the person who is ministered to; they are a blessing to God himself. At the heart of all our acts of kindness should be a desire to show our love for Jesus by showing love to others in all walks of life – the sick, the poor, the needy, the hungry.

Down through history, many Christian women have pioneered in this area, often going against worldly values, provoking criticism, even endangering their lives. For example:

PIONEERS

- Elizabeth Fry (prison work)
- Mother Teresa (ministering to the poor in Calcutta)
- Jackie Pullinger-To (working among drug addicts in Hong Kong)
- Florence Nightingale

What others can you think of?

What a tradition to follow in! The beauty of it is that we do not need to be especially gifted to be kind – we simply work out the love of God where we are.

PRAY

1. For God's strategy to reach areas which know nothing of the love of God.

2. For opportunities to be kind.

3. For more resources to show kindness.

Chapter 8

Submission to our husbands

Section One: What Is Biblical Submission?

INTRODUCTION

The last instruction in our study is about being subject to our husbands. It is interesting that this is separated from the first instruction, i.e. to love our husbands. Although the two things are linked, I believe Paul wants us to examine this issue separately. It is fundamental to our Christian beliefs and has far-reaching implications.

Before we look specifically at submission to our husbands, we need to understand a basic principle – that of spiritual authority.

THE 'S' WORD

What is your reaction to the word 'submission'? Do you love it or loathe it? Does it provoke anger? Cynicism? Frustration? Or a sense of well-being and security?

Many react violently, yet the Bible shows it is a beautiful, desirable quality. Why do you think it provokes negative feelings?

One reason is that the word has become debased through wrong usage. People think they know what it means, but like other gifts and attributes of God, it has become weakened and distorted. The enemy robs it of its power by lies and caricatures. Take the words 'holy', 'love' and 'meek'. We bring to these words a superficial understanding which owes more to modern usage than their true origins.

So we set up a caricature which we rightly hate. What flashes into your mind when you hear the word 'submission'? Some people have said that it brings to mind a dog coming to heel, or a victorious wrestler with his foot on his opponent's neck.

Another reason why submission provokes negative feelings is that human nature rebels against the whole idea of it. Ever since the Fall, mankind has desired independence, self-assertion and self-indulgence. 'Me' is the centre of my universe.

But we were not created to be like that. We were created to relate to God, to glorify him. Our conversion is the beginning of a process of restoring God's purpose of having him at the centre of our lives.

Before exploring the part that submission plays in this process, we need to lay a foundation on which to build our thinking. How does God think? What are his ways? How does human wisdom differ from his? Are we prepared to abandon our concepts if necessary and embrace new ways of thinking?

THE WISDOM OF GOD (I CORINTHIANS 1:18–31)

Two examples of man's wisdom are found in verse 22:

1. The Jews wanted signs

That is, they wanted visible, tangible events. To them, wisdom lay in satisfying a need to see with their own eyes – 'If I see I'll believe!' (as Doubting Thomas).

Many would agree with this position as it seems to make sense. We judge by what we see and hear. But Jesus said, 'Even if one were to rise from the dead, they will not believe.'

Of themselves, signs do not make us wise or bring us to God (v.21). They can point to Jesus, but cannot save us.

2. The Greeks searched for wisdom

They revelled in debate and philosophical discussion. They wanted to arrive at truth by intellectual brilliance. In fact they enjoyed the process of debate so much it would become an end in itself, and Paul warns against being 'captivated' by the fascination of empty philosophy.

SO WHAT IS GOD'S WISDOM?

1. A message (v.21)

God has spoken. He has declared a way of salvation. 'Salvation' does not only mean saving our souls from eternal damnation; it contains the sense of 'salvage' – rescue, restore, reclaim. In other words, it's about a different way of living; it's about knowing God. It's not only about how we get in, but how we go on.

So God's wisdom, God's message, goes on being relevant to us.

His wisdom is not proved by miracles (although they can back it up), nor is it arrived at by clever human logic.

God has spoken. His wisdom is fixed.

2. A man

How did Jesus model God's wisdom? In Isaiah we find the prophecy about the Messiah (Is 11:1–5). Verse 2 says: 'The Spirit of the Lord will rest on him.'

QUESTIONS

1. What are the characteristics of the Spirit (v.2)?

2. What will be his delight (v.3)?

3. How will he make decisions (v.3)?

Jesus, full of wisdom, would not judge by appearance or hearsay. He would not make independent decisions based on external criteria; he would choose to obey God.

Jesus also modelled God's wisdom by his attitude (Phil 2). He was equal with God, but chose to lay aside the privileges that he was entitled to. He became a servant, choosing to be subservient to a master. He laid aside independence and initiative, choosing instead to love the Father's will and to do it.

This pathway led to death on the cross. Because of his obedience, God exalted and honoured him.

In 1 John 2:6 it says that if we claim to have fellowship with him, we must walk as he walked. The things that particularly characterised Jesus' 'walk' were submission and authority, meekness and majesty, and humility and power.

Example: The healing of the paralytic (John 5)

Multitudes of rich folk were waiting to be healed. What would you do? Human wisdom (judging on the basis of what our ears and eyes tell us) would probably suggest one of the following:

- Turn and run.
- Go home and pray.
- Work your way round the pool, laying hands on and praying with people.
- Try to select the most deserving causes.

What did Jesus do (v.19)? He listened to the Father, and did what the Father said. He went to one man who had been crippled for thirty-eight years and ordered him to stand up and walk.

Jesus did not argue, he just obeyed. His obedience gave him authority.

Do you want to be a woman who acts with God's authority? The root of Jesus' authority was submission to the Father. Submission is the essence of the Christian life for every believer.

SUBMISSION TO WHAT OR WHOM?

1. The word of God
Recognising that this is our highest authority, we choose to believe it and obey it.

'Every word of God is flawless' (Prov 30:5–6).

'The word of God stands for ever' (1 Pet 1:25).

'Prophecy [of Scripture] never had its origin in the will of man, but men spoke from God as they were carried along by the Holy Spirit' (2 Pet 1:21).

'Your word is a lamp to my feet and a light for my path' (Ps 119:105).

'The law of the Lord is perfect, reviving the soul. The statutes of the Lord are trustworthy' (Ps 19:7).

2. Those appointed by God to govern the church
See Hebrews 13:17; 1 Thessalonians 5:12–13 and 1 Timothy 5:17.

3. One another
'Submit to one another out of reverence for Christ' (Eph 5:21).

4. Servants to masters
Today's equivalent would be an employee to his boss.

'Obey earthly masters with respect and fear, and with sincerity of heart, just as you would obey Christ' (Eph 6:5–7). See also Colossians 3:22–25.

5. Secular authority
See 1 Peter 2:13; 1 Timothy 1:1–3 and Titus 3:1–2.
 Read Romans 13:1–6.
 Who establishes secular authority (v.1)?
 What will happen if you rebel (v.2)?
 Why else should we submit to the authorities (v.5)?

6. Children to parents
See Ephesians 6:1–3 and Colossians 3:20.

7. Young men to older men
See 1 Peter 5:5.

8. Wives to husbands
See Ephesians 5:22–24; Colossians 3:18; Titus 2:5 and 1 Peter 3:1–6.

What is abundantly clear from these passages and many others is that God is looking for an atmosphere of humility that should pervade the whole church.

 Self-seeking is completely foreign to the ethos of the church. Instead we should be displaying an eagerness to love and serve one another, looking for opportunities to help and encourage each other. The foundation of this is not some legalistic teaching about submission that talks about position, hierarchy, inferiority and so on. It is that Jesus himself has laid down his life for us, and wants us to lay down our lives for one another, out of love and gratitude.

THE POWER OF SUBMISSION

Something that our enemy knows all too well, but which we often forget, is that submission is very powerful when it is motivated by loving obedience.

 Was Jesus powerful? We know he was. He was utterly fearless. He strode into the temple courts and overturned the tables of the money-changers, denouncing their greedy preoccupations in a place that should have been devoted to prayer. He confronted the hypocrisy of the Pharisees and was unafraid to touch lepers. He defied the proprieties of the day by being seen with undesirable people. He cast out demons, healed the sick and raised the dead. What power! What authority! Isn't he wonderful?

How did he do this? As we have seen, he was totally in submission to the Father. He worked with him in complete harmony. The devil was always trying to divide the Father and Son, to make the Son act independently. That was what the temptations were all about: trying to get Jesus to strike out on his own; do his own thing. But Jesus never gave in. If he had, he would not have been the perfect, obedient, spotless Lamb that was needed to bear our sin.

He always worked in total co-operation with the Father. So submission is really all about saying 'no' to my ways and 'yes' to God's. That's powerful and that's why the devil hates it.

Do you want authority in God's kingdom? You can only get it his way – the way of the cross.

Section Two: Working It Out

Once we have established the principle of submission as seen in Jesus' relationship to the Father, we have to learn to work it out. Submission is at the heart of Christianity.

QUESTION

Wives are specifically called to submit to their husbands (Eph 5:21–24; Col 3:18; Titus 2:4).

With what attitude should we do this?

When we submit to our husbands it is an expression of our obedience to Jesus. He is our example.

WHAT SUBMISSION IS NOT

1. Passive
Wives are instructed to be subject to their husbands as the church is to Christ (Eph 5:24). The church has been given many commands to fulfil in bringing in the kingdom of God. She must be strong and vital, actively obedient to Christ.

2. Lazy
Some people see submission as a 'cop-out', a convenient way of opting out of responsibility or making decisions. We must not use submission as a cover for dithering, or not getting involved.

3. The doormat syndrome

Many fear submission because they think that all self-expression and personhood will be denied them, and they will become stunted and never realise their potential. Jesus was not a nothing, and he does not intend us to be. We are to submit to our husbands 'as to the Lord', that is in faith, that as we aim to please him we will mature and become more like him.

4. Silent

We are to 'build up one another in love', 'encourage one another', 'agree with one another', 'admonish one another', and pray with one another. The wife is God's partner for her husband and he needs her wisdom, support and counsel (Prov 31:26). But it is her attitude in doing this that is so important. A woman can bring valid counsel to her husband, but she can either do it in a way that dishonours him, or she can do it respectfully.

5. Manipulative

Trying to get your own way by subtle manoeuvres is an abuse of submission. Jesus did not seek to please the Father with the secret motive of getting his own way. He did his Father's will because he loved it (Jn 4:34), and that was enough. Do you love your husband like that?

QUESTION

Can you think of some things to do that delight your husband? Loving gestures should be an end in themselves, not a means of getting your own way.

---

6. Weak

It often takes courage to submit. We feel safe when we are in control, and sometimes it is hard to hand over the reins.

7. Legalistic

Submission is not something you do to earn approval and acceptance from God, and it certainly should not be demanded by a domineering husband. If it is, then he has not understood the heart of the gospel, that is, a love relationship which involves sacrificial living. This in fact is what is required of him – that he love his wife as Jesus loved the church (Eph 5:25).

8. Yielding to intimidation

You may be asking: What if my husband is domineering and demanding? How should I act towards him?

God does not want you to be crushed, and he does not expect you to take uncomplainingly a husband's actions that are wrong. Submission should never damage our conscience.

In 1 Samuel 25 we find the story of a beautiful, intelligent woman called Abigail, married to a mean, surly man named Nabal. David's men protected Nabal's men at sheep-shearing time, but Nabal refused to acknowledge their help and goodwill. In reply to a request from David for some well-earned food, he not only denied them any, but sent a rude and offensive message.

Incensed, David was about to retaliate by sending over 400 armed men to teach him a lesson. Abigail heard of his plan. She did not adopt a passive attitude to her husband's meanness, or to David's angry response. She acted swiftly, by bringing a generous gift to David. Her action disarmed him and averted a crisis and much bloodshed.

Our first duty is to obey God, and if there is a conflict between obeying him and our husband, God must come first.

We are not to let our husband walk over us. We are to be respectful but not fearful: 'You are her [Sarah's] daughters if you do what is right and do not give way to fear' (1 Pet 3:6).

The next verse (1 Pet 3:7) instructs husbands to 'be considerate as you live with your wives, and treat them with respect ... heirs with you'. If they do not, that 'fellow-heir' needs to point it out, for her husband is putting himself in a position where his prayers will not be answered!

In the final analysis, a one-sided marriage is frustrating and unfulfilling to both parties. A dominated wife must seek the grace and courage to speak firmly and clearly to her husband. Obviously this could be extremely hard if he is not prepared to listen. We would hope that if he is a Christian man, he would be open to correction. This is where an objective third party, such as an elder or trained marriage counsellor, could give invaluable assistance. Ideally, in the church we should be developing close relationships where friends can speak into one another's lives and marriages.

Be encouraged by 1 Peter 3:1–2: 'If any of them [husbands] do not believe the word, they may be won over without words by the behaviour of their wives, when they see the purity and reverence of your lives.'

What Peter is saying here is that *attitude* will go a long way towards winning over a non-Christian husband. Being loving, gentle, supportive and seeking to please him as far as the wife can without injuring her conscience could be more effective than arguing, cajoling or preaching at him!

Each wife must work out in the context of her own marriage and walk with God how she can let her love for God overflow and strengthen her love and respect for her husband.

It might be encouraging to find a friend in a similar position and pray together for the husbands.

WHAT SUBMISSION IS

1. Voluntary
Philippians 2 shows us that Jesus made the choice of laying aside his privileges and becoming a servant. Wives are told to *submit themselves* (Eph 5:22). It is not a matter of coercion but of choosing God's way.

2. Joyful
Jesus was not grudging about doing the Father's will. It was his 'meat' (Jn 4:34). Isaiah prophesied, 'He will delight in

the fear of the Lord (11:3). He maintained this attitude right up to the cross. In the Garden of Gethsemane he faced it again. Could he still embrace his Father's will? It was an agonising decision to drink that cup (Lk 22:42). Yet he made it for 'the joy set before him' (Heb 12:2).

3. Positive
The will of God is 'good, pleasing and perfect' (Rom 12:2). To find the will of God and do it brings about good in your life. To submit to your husband is a positive act of obedience.

4. An expression of trust
See Proverbs 31:10–12. To invest your energies in pleasing your husband creates a bond of trust. If you can't trust, you can't submit. If there are areas where you do not trust your husband, this needs to be prayed over and talked about with him and/or a counsellor.

5. Powerful
The enemy hates submission because it is Christ-like. When we are submitting to God we have authority: 'Submit yourselves, then, to God. Resist the devil' (Jas 4:7). Satan does everything he can to pervert submission. People under the lordship of Christ, submissive to his will, are dangerous.

6. Painful
See Luke 9:23 and Philippians 2.
(a) The cross is the ultimate in submission. Jesus had to decide if he could abandon himself to death and trust the Father to raise him up (Acts 2:27).
(b) Jesus said that we must take up our cross. The cross hurts. Today we try to avoid pain at all costs. If there is pain we rush to alleviate it – not only physically, but emotionally and spiritually. But some pain is not only unavoidable, but necessary. Laying down our wills is sometimes painful, but don't side-step the pain. Let it do God's work in you to purify you.

(c) The cross is not only painful, it is fatal. Sometimes the 'hurt' involved in submission is simply a case of bruised ego. The ego must actually die, not be carefully preserved (Col 3:5, 12–14; Eph 4:22–24).

All through our lives, God will call us to obey him over various issues, e.g. speaking to a neighbour about Jesus, praying for someone who is sick, giving away money, fasting for a day or two, refusing to lie. There are countless ways in which we will learn to respond to him in obedience.

They may often appear illogical; they will go against the tide of what we regard as 'normal'. They may even seem suicidal inasmuch as they are the opposite to what caution or common sense would advise!

But whatever we do for God must be done in faith. Faith pleases God. Faith says, 'However stupid this seems, if God told me to do it, it must be effective.' Mary was a prime example of this when she said, 'Behold the handmaid of the Lord. Let it be to me according to your word.'

It is also interesting to note Esther's example. She was obedient to her foster father (Esther 2:20), co-operative with authority in the palace (Esther 2:8–9,15) and submissive to her husband. But this was paralleled by a steady rise in confidence and authority.

In the end a wife's submission is not only to her husband, but to God and to his plan for marriage. It is resting, leaning, trusting and abandoning yourself to the Lord, in total confidence that his way is the best, kindest and most fruitful.

THE NITTY GRITTY!

There are many huge issues in marriage which require the husband and wife to make a decision. For example, where to live, financial priorities and principles, changes of career, the children's education.

Often it's the smaller things that test our commitment to submission. For example, where to go on holiday, having the in-laws at Christmas, arranging the furniture or choosing what to watch on TV.

Probably (hopefully!) there are many areas of life about which you agree. There will, however, be some areas about which you differ. Let's attempt to define these.

1. Personal preferences

I like trout, but Terry prefers steak. Since neither appears on our table with any frequency this is not much of a problem! Most couples find that they learn to accommodate each other's preferences, make allowances and adapt. This is part of the maturing process, where give and take come into play.

> **QUESTION**
>
> **Many things on which we differ are simply not worth making an issue of.**
>
> **Can you think of some examples?**

2. Irritating mannerisms

Careful! Irritating to whom? If it's only you, maybe it's you who needs to change. If it's an ongoing habit which you can't bear, which also embarrasses others, pick a good moment to introduce the subject, and do it gently. Don't go on and on! Submission does not mean you have to like everything about him. No doubt there are areas which need improvement and sometimes he may have to listen to you and change. (See Proverbs 19:13; 21:9.)

3. Big differences

Problems with money, leisure time and disciplining the children can fall into this category. A wife can be afraid of submitting to a husband in money matters if he appears irresponsible. They need to check whether or not they are handling finances according to scriptural principles. If they are, the wife need not fear. If not, they must be humble enough to discuss their goals and aims, maybe with a responsible third party present.

Similarly, disciplining the children is something the couple need to agree upon, using Scripture as their guide. They need to be aware of each other's vulnerable areas (e.g. the wife being too 'soft', the husband being too lazy) and address them. But ultimately the husband as the head must take the responsibility for making sure it's done, and the wife must let him. It is the husband's responsibility to make sure the family is properly ordered, but both must work at this.

4. Character deficiencies

As the rosy glow of the honeymoon wears off, each partner may be dismayed to find the other isn't as perfect as they previously expected! 'How can I submit to him when he's lazy/selfish, he snores/won't talk/doesn't understand?'

Give him time! He's learning too! Give him love, support and respect. Let him know that you want to submit to him; that your attitude is to live for his good (Prov 31:10).

Keep remembering to honour him. There will be times when it seems hard because he appears to be making the wrong decisions for the wrong reasons. By all means talk about it, but let your attitude be humble. If your husband is walking with God, he will want to get it right too. He won't be able to develop his ability to lead if you keep pulling the rug out from under his feet; neither will you feel secure and safe if you always insist on making the decisions.

> **QUESTION**
>
> Now be honest: what are your character deficiencies?

5. Different temperaments

I tend to be impulsive, spontaneous, intuitive. Terry is more even-tempered, cautious, logical – and yes, wiser! Sometimes I have felt frustrated and impatient with his more measured, objective responses. But I have also learned that in the end he is nearly always right. I have not suffered by submitting, but have gained the priceless gift of being loved, secure and protected.

Early on, I believed Psalm 128:4 – 'Thus is the man blessed who fears the Lord.' My husband fears God, so the promises that follow apply to him and to me.

> **QUESTION**
>
> God often puts a man and wife of differing temperaments together.
>
> What are the advantages and the disadvantages?

TO SUM UP

Basically, many women fear submission because they fear losing control or their identity. In the beginning God intended, and created, two people living in harmony. This was spoiled when the woman, lured by Satan, disobeyed God, and their unity was disrupted. Thus, 'going your own way', 'doing your own thing', self-assertion, dissension and disagreement became the norm.

Then God in Christ reconciled us with himself, and made it possible for us to live in harmony with one another. In Christian marriage God is restoring his original plan where the man and woman are to live in a secure, loving, fulfilling relationship, the man being the head, and the woman the helper.

As we seek to work out God's restoration programme, we shall be changed, and we can play a part in changing our bit of the world as we live out the values of the kingdom of God.

Recommended Reading

Atkins, Anne. *Split Image*. Hodder

Virgo, Wendy. *Women Set Free*. Kingsway Publications

Ed. Lees, Shirley. *The Role of Women*. IVP

The baptism in the Holy Spirit

If you are a new Christian, it may be that you have not yet had the baptism in the Holy Spirit explained to you. Jesus told his disciples that after he had ascended, he would send the Holy Spirit to them to be with them for ever. The Holy Spirit would be another one like him; he would dwell in them, lead them into truth, teach them and remind them of the things Jesus had said. Jesus described him as 'the promise of the Father' and said he would empower them to be witnesses to him. Witnessing simply means spreading the news about him in word and deed. The disciples were desolate that Jesus would be physically going away from them, but he told them that when the Spirit came, it would be even better for them, because they would be able to do the things he did and more of them.

HOW DID THE HOLY SPIRIT COME?

Acts 2

Jesus 'ascended on high' and sent him. The disciples, 120 of them, were all waiting expectantly gathered in a room in Jerusalem (Acts 2). Suddenly the sound of a great rushing wind filled the room and they saw flames above each other's heads. They knew they were being filled with power. Their bodies could hardly take the impact and they acted almost like drunken men. They probably staggered. Some may have fallen.

They all began to praise God and then realised they were speaking in many different languages which they had never learned. Excited, they spilled onto the street outside. Jerusalem was full of visitors who had come for the feast of Pentecost. A large crowd quickly gathered and Peter seized the opportunity. With boldness and impassioned vigour, he preached the gospel. Such was the impact of his preaching that his hearers were cut to the heart. 'What must we do?' they cried.

'Believe on the Lord Jesus Christ, be baptised and you shall receive the Holy Spirit, promised to all God calls,' he replied. Three thousand did so.

The early church was launched. Right from the start, the preaching of the gospel included the expectation that new converts would also be filled with the Holy Spirit.

Acts 8

Philip went to Samaria and preached. Many responded and people were healed. When the apostles heard that people were becoming Christians in Samaria, they sent Peter and John to them. When they arrived they prayed for them that they might receive the Holy Spirit, because although they had been baptised in water, they had not yet been baptised in the Holy Spirit. Then Peter and John laid hands on them and they received the Holy Spirit. We don't know exactly what they saw, but something dramatic must have happened because a man called Simon the Sorcerer, when he saw that the Holy Spirit was given by the laying on of the apostles' hands, offered them money and said, 'Give me also this ability so that everyone on whom I lay my hands may receive the Holy Spirit' (v.19). Peter answered very sternly that this was not a gift that could be bought.

So we can see from this account that the baptism in the Spirit was something that they expected to happen soon after people were saved and it was accompanied by some dramatic sign. On this occasion it was passed on through the laying on of hands.

Acts 9

Saul, a persecutor of the church, had a dramatic encounter with Jesus on the Damascus Road. His life was totally changed. Three days later, a Christian called Ananias laid hands on him and he was baptised in the Holy Spirit. We know Paul spoke in tongues because he says so elsewhere in the New Testament, but whether or not it happened immediately he was baptised in the Holy Spirit we are not told. All we know is that it happened soon after his conversion, that hands were laid upon him and that at some point he also spoke in tongues, as well as using other gifts of the Holy Spirit.

Acts 10

Here we have the account of Peter preaching the gospel to the first Gentile converts, a group of Romans in Caesarea. The Holy Spirit fell upon them without human agency while Peter was still preaching, and they spoke in tongues and prophesied.

Acts 19

This is the account of what happened when Paul preached the gospel to a group in Ephesus. He found some disciples and asked them, 'Did you receive the Holy Spirit when you believed?'

They answered, 'No, we have not even heard that there is a Holy Spirit.'

These people had not yet had the gospel clearly preached to them. They had only heard John the Baptist preaching the message of repentance. So Paul preached the gospel of Jesus. On hearing this, they were baptised into the name of Jesus. When Paul laid hands on them, the Holy Spirit came on them and they spoke in tongues and prophesied.

WHAT CAN WE LEARN FROM THESE ACCOUNTS?

1. The baptism of the Holy Spirit is related to conversion. All these people either received the Holy Spirit at conversion, or

very soon after. The baptism of the Holy Spirit was not the same thing as being born again, but something that the early Christians expected to happen soon after someone was born again.

2. It was often given through the laying on of hands, but not always. God often uses a third party when someone wants to be filled with the Holy Spirit. An invitation may be made in a meeting for people to come forward for prayer. Then the preacher and/or elders or ministry team will pray with those who respond by gently laying their hands on their heads and asking the Holy Spirit to come.

Can anyone 'lay on hands' and pray like this? In Acts 8, Philip sent for Peter and John, the apostles, to come and do it.

In Acts 9, an unknown believer named Ananias laid hands on Paul.

The Bible doesn't seem particularly fussy about it. It seems to be an area where believers can minister to one another as the body of Christ.

In Acts 10, the Holy Spirit fell while Peter was still preaching with no human agency at all. That often happens today and I have known many people receive the Spirit on their own at home, or while walking in the country, lying in bed, or even in the bathroom!

3. It was often accompanied by speaking in tongues, but again, this was not referred to on every occasion. But we can deduce that they expected to receive speaking in tongues or other gifts of the Holy Spirit either at the time of being baptised in the Spirit, or soon after.

This is a wonderful, precious gift, often devalued. It enables us to communicate with God, spirit to Spirit. When we run out of our own language or can't think what to pray, the Holy Spirit helps us. Sometimes, as Romans 8 tells us, we may feel deeply moved in prayer, but the Spirit can interpret even wordless longings.

Often it is a wonderful joyous release of adoration, especially when our hearts are so full we cannot express what we feel. It is truly like rivers of water pouring from our innermost beings.

Speaking in tongues is not something God does to us. We use our normal speech apparatus – larynx, teeth, tongue, lips – as in any speech. Many supernatural events in the Bible require a human response to a word from God. Then God comes and does what we cannot do. For example, we read of a widow who had only a tiny amount of oil left in a bottle. Starvation was staring her in the face. Elisha the prophet told her to collect as many vessels as she could. So she ran around to her neighbours and borrowed all that could be found. Elisha told her to start pouring out oil. She began to pour out what she had – and miraculously it just kept flowing until all the vessels were filled.

It would not have happened if she had sat and waited for a miracle. She had to act in faith by giving what she had. This is a good picture of speaking in tongues.

The enemy always challenges people when they start speaking in tongues. He uses the same old trick, 'Is it the real thing?' Don't take any notice of him. His purpose is to stop Jesus being worshipped and you being built up by introducing doubt. The truth is, you couldn't do it before, now you can. The Bible tells us that speaking in tongues edifies us, so keep doing it (1 Cor 14:4).

WATER FOR THE THIRSTY

'Jesus stood and said in a loud voice, "If anyone is thirsty, let him come to me and drink. Whoever believes in me, as the Scripture has said, streams of living water will flow from within him." By this he meant the Spirit, whom those who believed in him were later to receive. Up to that time the Spirit had not been given, since Jesus had not yet been glorified' (Jn 7:37).

This scripture helps us to understand how to receive the Holy Spirit. First, we come to Jesus. He invites thirsty people to come to him. We do not come to a method or a well-known preacher; we come to Jesus, just like when we first became a Christian.

Second, we must be thirsty! When you are thirsty you need a drink. The Holy Spirit is not an optional extra. He is totally vital to us. We can't live without water and we can't live the Christian life without the Holy Spirit. Come to Jesus and drink.

Third, he is proof that Jesus is risen, ascended and glorified. If anyone had come to Jesus that day when Jesus was making the invitation, he would have had to say, 'Wait a little while. I'll send him when I'm glorified.' Now Jesus is in heaven and has made the Holy Spirit available to all believers.

So, when a thirsty person responds to Jesus' invitation to come to him and drink, and he floods them with the Holy Spirit, it is a further demonstration and proof that he is alive and glorified.

KEEP BEING FILLED

Our first experience of having the Holy Spirit come on us is known as the baptism in the Spirit ('baptism' is a word associated with new beginnings), but it is not intended to be the only time. Just like we need to keep drinking water, we need to keep being filled with the Spirit (Eph 5:18). So come to Jesus and ask him to fill you every day with his living water, the Holy Spirit.

The use of corporal punishment

HOW SHOULD IT BE USED?

1. Sparingly

It is not the first resort, or the only one. It is one of the ways of training indicated in the book of Proverbs. Warning, guiding and instructing are continually spoken of. But we cannot ignore the explicit references to the use of the rod, so there are occasions when it is appropriate.

2. With control

It is not to be seen as a time for parents to vent their anger or frustration on the child, however provoking he or she may have been. It is an opportunity to train. If you are angry, wait until your anger cools. Be careful, calm and deliberate.

3. With love

'The Lord disciplines those he loves, and he punishes everyone he accepts as a son' (Heb 12:6). As we have already noted, true discipline is a mark of sonship and acceptance. Any form of discipline must be undertaken with love as a motivating factor, and this includes the rod. The child must know he or she is still loved, even during the process of discipline. We were careful to say to our children as we went to fetch the spoon from the drawer, 'Son (or Anna), I don't enjoy doing this any more than you like receiving it. But I love you and I want you to grow up straight, not crooked.'

One day, when Anna was about three, she was skipping along the street holding my husband Terry's hand. She looked up at him smiling and said, 'What comes after spanking?'

'You tell me!' he said.

'Hugs!' she replied gleefully.

4. With faith

'No discipline seems pleasant at the time, but painful. Later on, however, it produces a harvest of righteousness and peace for those who have been trained by it' (Heb 12:11).

While you are dealing with an incident, it is hard to keep in mind the long-term view. You wish your child would not disobey. You hate to get the wooden spoon out again; you hate to have to go through the process again. He is crying; you feel like crying. It takes time and emotional energy. You are tempted to skip it this time; turn a blind eye, forget it. It is at this point that you have to ask yourself, 'Why am I doing this?' And the answer should be something like, 'Because I love God, and I love my child.' We show our love to God by doing things his way, believing they are fruitful. He is a loving parent to us, and disciplines us when necessary – carefully, patiently and consistently.

5. In private

This is not an exercise in public humiliation. Whenever possible, take the child aside into another room and shut the door and deal with him in private.

6. With clarity

It is vital that the child knows the parameters you have set, and where he has overstepped them. We must not use the rod if our child has acted in ignorance or confusion. On the other hand, don't be manipulated into letting them off the hook!

7. A rod, not the hand

It is better for children to associate punishment with a neutral object such as a wooden spoon. Let the hand be associated with blessing, comforting and caressing (Is 10:5).

When the punishment is delivered it should be hard enough to sting otherwise it is pointless. The best place is the child's bottom where there is plenty of padding! Take heart from Proverbs 23:13 – he will not die ... though he may yell enough to make you think he will! Actually, it is not good to allow children to scream uncontrollably. Talk calmly and try to calm them down.

We began at about the age of two years. In our experience, toddlers of two and three needed the spoon with tedious regularity, sometimes more than once a day! I did not enjoy it and was often tempted to give it up. However, I discovered that there were phases when they played up and needed it more, and then quiet periods. Of course it varied from child to child, some being stronger willed than others. It is difficult to quantify, but by the age of five it was comparatively seldom, and reserved for flagrant breaches of obedience. I think we very rarely, if ever, spanked a child as old as twelve.

Bear in mind that the amount of space devoted to this subject here is disproportionate to the amount of time we have given to other topics, but it is a controversial issue today and needs careful consideration. In our family life, far more time was spent in laughing together, having fun, playing, hugging, holding hands. The wooden spoon had its place but it was just a part of the tapestry of family life. The following is an anecdote to illustrate that using the rod is a useful tool for teaching truth about guilt and forgiveness.

We have a large field behind our house, an ideal area for energetic children to play and throw balls. It was therefore unnecessary for them to kick or throw balls around in our garden area. I wanted to keep the flower beds from being trampled and to protect the neighbours' greenhouse! So we banned ball-play in the garden.

One day, Ben disobeyed. There was an ominous crash as a ball smashed a window. Ben went to the kitchen drawer, took out the spoon and went to his father. 'I'm sorry, Dad, I threw a ball and broke a window.' Ben was guilty, and he wanted his guilt dealt with. Lying, denying, attempting to cover up ... none of these would have worked.

Terry took him into the study and shut the door. He told Ben to bend over, and he spanked him. Tearfully, Ben straightened up, saying, 'Sorry, Dad.'

Terry hugged him. 'OK, son, it's over. Don't play with your ball in the garden again! I forgive you. Now let's pray and ask God to forgive you too.'

This true story illustrates several points.

1. Children need to face guilt, not evade it.
2. Ben was disciplined for disobeying, not for breaking a window.
3. He understood that his disobedience resulted in breaking a window, and therefore the ban on throwing balls in the garden was reasonable.
4. He welcomed the use of the spoon as punishment. It dealt with his guilt more effectively than angry words, sarcasm, silence or a lecture would have done.
5. When it was over, it was over. True, Terry still had to have the window reglazed, but not at the expense of alienation from Ben, and a bad atmosphere that could have continued for days.

We often found that after the wooden spoon the children seemed freer, happier and more affectionate than before. They felt accepted.